MASTERS OF ART

PABLO PICASSO

Stefano Loria

◆

ILLUSTRATED BY

Simone Boni

L.R. Galante

PETER BEDRICK BOOKS

NEW YORK

DoGi

Produced by
Donati Giudici Associati, Florence
Original title:
Pablo Picasso
Text:
Stefano Loria
Illustrations:
Simone Boni
L.R. Galante
Picture research and coordination of
co-editions:
Caroline Godard
Art direction:
Oliviero Ciriaci
Sebastiano Ranchetti
Page design:
Laura Davis
Editing:
Enza Fontana
English translation:
Deborah Misuri-Charkham
Editor, English-language edition:
Ruth Nason
Typesetting:
Ken Alston – A.J.Latham Ltd

© 1995 Donati Giudici Associati s.r.l.
Florence, Italy
English language text © 1995 by
Macdonald Young Books/
Peter Bedrick Books

Library of Congress Cataloging-in-
Publication Data

Loria, Stefano.
Picasso / Stefano Loria: illustrated
by Simone Boni, L.R. Galante.
p. cm. – (Masters of art)
Includes index.
ISBN 0-87226-318-5
1. Picasso, Pablo, 1881-1973 –
Criticism and interpretation. I. Boni,
Simone. II. Galante, L.R. III. Title.
IV. Series: Masters of art
(Peter Bedrick Books)
N6853.P5L69 1995
709'.2—dc20   95-31830
                              CIP

Printed by *Conti Tipocolor*,
Calenzano (Florence)

Photolitho:
Professional D.T.P Venanzoni s.r.l.,
Florence

Second edition, 1998

◆ HOW THE INFORMATION IS PRESENTED

Every double-page spread is a chapter in its own right, devoted to an aspect of the life and art of Picasso or the major artistic and cultural developments of his time. The text at the top of the left-hand page (1) and the central illustration are concerned with this main theme. The text in italics (2) gives a chronological account of events in Picasso's life. The other material (photographs, paintings and drawings) enlarges on the central theme.

Some pages focus on major works by Picasso. They include the following information: (1) an account of the painting's history; (2) a description of the content and imagery of the work; (3) a critical analysis and detailed examination of its formal aspects. There are also reproductions of works by other artists, to set Picasso's work in its historical context and demonstrate its originality.

CONTENTS

CONTEMPORARIES

♦ **PABLO RUIZ PICASSO** (1881-1973)
In accordance with Spanish custom, Pablo had two surnames: his father's, Ruiz, and his mother's, Picasso. At first he signed his works as Pablo Ruiz, but began to use the name Pablo Picasso at the turn of the century. Although quite short, Pablo was strong and well-built with a "mirada fuerte", magnetic eyes.

Pablo Picasso must certainly be the most famous artist of our times. This painter, sculptor, potter, graphic artist, poet and campaigner for peace produced works which changed the course of painting and sculpture in the twentieth century by creating new ways of representing reality. Born in Málaga, Spain, he moved to Paris, art capital of the world, in the early 1900s. He was a man of great energy and enormous talent. He forged close friendships with poets and writers including Guillaume Apollinaire and Jean Cocteau, and, together with painters such as Henri Matisse, Georges Braque and Joan Miró, started some of the most important modern art movements. The most revolutionary of these was Cubism, of which *Les Demoiselles d'Avignon* (1907) is an example. The name Picasso became the very symbol of modern art.

OLGA KOKLOVA ♦
(1891-1955)
Picasso's first wife was a Russian ballerina with the Sergei Diaghilev company.

♦ **DORA MAAR**
(born 1907)
A painter and photographer, the most intellectual woman Picasso loved.

JEAN COCTEAU ♦
(1889-1963)
A poet and playwright and great friend of Picasso. He frequented cultural salons in Paris where he emerged as one of the most brilliant literary talents in twentieth-century France.

♦ **GEORGES BRAQUE**
(1882-1963)
This great craftsman of painting invented original techniques and was one of the finest artists of Cubism.

♦ **HENRI MATISSE**
(1869-1954)
A painter and sculptor, he left his job in a law firm to concentrate on art and became one of the greatest masters of modern painting.

ANDRÉ BRETON ♦
(1896-1966)
A writer with a charismatic personality, who founded the Surrealist movement. His literary theories deeply influenced contemporary art.

DANIEL-HENRI ♦
KAHNWEILER
(1884-1979)
Picasso's trusted art dealer was an extremely capable former banker. He launched Cubism on the international market.

JACQUELINE ROQUE ♦
(1926-1986)
Picasso's second wife was a loyal and understanding companion during the last twenty years of the painter's life. She loved and greatly admired him.

PAULO PICASSO ♦
(1921-1975)
Picasso's first child, born during his marriage to Olga Koklova. Picasso had three more children: Maya, Claude and Paloma.

FERNANDE OLIVIER ♦
(1881-1966)
Picasso's companion during his first years in Paris.

JAUME SABARTÈS ♦
(1881-1968)
A friend since 1899, he became Picasso's personal secretary in 1935.

♦ **MARIE-THÉRÈSE WALTER**
(1909-1977)
Picasso fell in love with her during the late 1920s. Tall, blonde and athletic, she kept her distance from the hustle and bustle of city life.

♦ **ANDRÉ MALRAUX**
(1901-1976)
A writer and friend of Picasso, in 1958 he became Minister of Cultural Affairs under Charles de Gaulle.

♦ **ANDRÉ SALMON**
(1881-1969)
A writer and one of Picasso's best friends while he was living in the Bateau Lavoir studio.

♦ **JOAN MIRÓ**
(1893-1983)
A Catalan painter and sculptor, part of the Surrealist movement.

♦ **MAX JACOB**
(1876-1944)
A poet and critic, interested in astrology, tarot cards and palmistry. He was good company and a fund of knowledge on all subjects, and so was a leading member of the group of friends with whom Picasso socialized in the early years in Paris.

♦ **GERTRUDE STEIN**
(1874-1946)
An American writer and a great collector and promoter of contemporary art.

PAUL ELUARD ♦
(1895-1952)
A poet belonging to the Surrealist group of writers. He and Picasso were close friends and shared a political objection to all war.

♦ **CARLOS CASAGEMAS**
(1881-1901)
An important friend of Picasso's youth, imaginative, sensitive and troubled. Aged twenty, he committed suicide because of an unhappy love affair.

♦ **AMBROISE VOLLARD**
(1865-1939)
He was one of the main art dealers at the beginning of the twentieth century. He was a cantankerous personality, but never failed to persuade collectors to buy his paintings.

♦ **FRANÇOISE GILOT**
(born 1922)
The daughter of a wealthy Parisian perfume manufacturer, she was Picasso's companion during the Second World War.

♦ **GUILLAUME APOLLINAIRE**
(1880-1918)
Poet, writer and critic, he was a brilliant and enthusiastic supporter of the modern painters and always at the center of disputes about art.

MÁLAGA

Málaga is a town by the Mediterranean Sea. At the time Picasso was born there, it was no longer prosperous as in previous centuries, when it had been an important trading port. However, people carried on with their traditional business activities and struggled with all the problems arising from the decline. The harbor still offered shelter to passing ships. Cotton was woven, there was a sugar refinery and wine was produced, although the profits made were less than before. A consequence of the economic downturn was that the cultural atmosphere of Málaga had become stagnant and provincial. The only noteworthy artistic institution was the San Telmo School of Fine Arts, which had been founded by royal decree in 1849. Among the teachers at the school were two painters from Valencia, Bernardo Fernández and Antonio Muñoz Degrain. Degrain was a friend of Pablo's father.

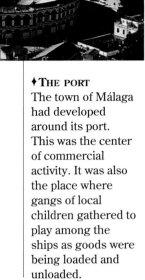

♦ **MOVING HOUSE**
Picasso spent his childhood in Málaga and his adolescence in La Coruña, on the north-west coast of Spain, and in Barcelona, on the eastern coast. Young Pablo had no difficulty in adapting to the changes in custom, climate and language that each move involved. Above: view of Málaga.

♦ **THE PORT**
The town of Málaga had developed around its port. This was the center of commercial activity. It was also the place where gangs of local children gathered to play among the ships as goods were being loaded and unloaded.

♦ **THE PIGEON-LOFT**
José Ruiz Blasco, 1878, oil on canvas, 102 x 147 cm (40 x 58 in) (Ayuntamiento, Málaga). Pablo's father painted the pigeons that flocked around the house.

♦ **PABLO'S DRAWING**
Pablo Picasso, *Pigeons*, 1890, pencil on paper, 11 x 22 cm (4$^{1/3}$ x 8$^{2/3}$ in) (Picasso Museum, Barcelona). Aged nine, Pablo drew the birds that interested his father.

♦ **HIS PARENTS**
José Ruiz Blasco (1838-1913), Picasso's father, was a merchant's son but had preferred art to business. In Málaga he taught drawing and painting at the School of Fine Arts and also worked for the municipal museum, restoring old canvases in poor condition. He was tall and fair-skinned and nicknamed "the Englishman" because of his blond hair. Although quite shy, he had a good sense of humor. He had two special interests: painting pigeons and going to the bullfight. Maria Picasso López (1855-1939) was seventeen years younger than her husband. She was optimistic and cheerful and never lost faith in her son's qualities. Even when times were hard, she offered him both moral and financial support and Pablo always had great affection for her.

♦ **PICASSO AND HIS SISTER, LOLA**
Lola was born in 1884. There was also another, younger, sister, Concepción, who contracted diphtheria when she was seven. Despite all efforts to save her, she died on 10 January 1895.

♦THE SCHOOL OF ART IN MÁLAGA
José Ruiz Blasco had studied at Málaga's San Telmo School of Fine Arts (center) himself. In 1879 he returned there as a qualified teacher of drawing and ornament. He received only a modest salary in this position.

♦A MAIN STREET IN LA CORUÑA
The art school in the town was built in 1889, commissioned by the aristocrat Eusebio Guarda. José Ruiz was a teacher there and his son Pablo a pupil, following regular courses. The teaching at the institute was traditional and academic.

♦TRAVELS
On a journey from Málaga to Barcelona, Pablo produced some small paintings recording his eight days on board ship. Pablo Picasso, *Valencia Marina*, 1895, oil on board, 10.1 x 15.5 cm (4 x 6 in) (Picasso Museum, Barcelona).

♦TWO FAVORITE SUBJECTS
Pablo Picasso, *Bullring and Pigeons*, c.1890, pencil on paper, 13.5 x 20.2 cm (5$^1/_3$ x 8 in) (Picasso Museum, Barcelona). Pablo had inherited his father's two main interests.

PICASSO THE STUDENT ♦
From the moment he began his art studies, Picasso was recognized as exceptionally talented. He was clearly a remarkable observer of life.

PICASSO'S LIFE

POWER OF ♦ EXPRESSION
Pablo Picasso, *Girl with Bare Feet*, 1895, oil on canvas, 75 x 50 cm (29$^1/_2$ x 19$^2/_3$ in) (Picasso Museum, Paris). Portraits painted by Picasso aged thirteen were works of art. His technical ability and powers of expression were already mature.

1. ♦ *Pablo Picasso was born on 25 October 1881 in Málaga, an old town by the sea in the far south of Spain. He was the son of two pure-blooded but very different Andalusians. José Ruiz Blasco, slim and quiet, was a painter and art teacher; Maria Picasso López was a plump and pleasant housewife. Pablo was a lively child. He reputedly learned to walk so that he could reach his favorite cookies, and he learned to draw at an early age and with extraordinary dedication, under his father's careful guidance. Despite the family's financial difficulties, Pablo's childhood was tranquil and he was surrounded by aunts and cousins who took care of him after the birth of his sister, Lola. In 1891, the whole family moved to La Coruña, a rainy town on the Atlantic coast. Picasso attended its Institute of Fine Arts where his father taught and where he received a traditional art training.* ❧➤

BARCELONA

♦ MODERNISME
Modernisme
stemmed from the
ideas of three Catalan
artists: Santiago
Rusiñol, Ramón
Casas and Miguel
Utrillo. Rusiñol's
painting followed
various styles in
different periods,
passing from realism
to symbolism. He was
also a writer and
organized cultural
projects. Casas tried
to combine his taste
for social realism
with a brilliant career
painting the portraits
of members of high
society. This activity
took him to the
USA, where he
was financially very
successful. Utrillo
was interested in
literature as well as
painting. All three
were friends of
Picasso and had an
influence on his
development as an
artist.

At the end of the nineteenth century, Barcelona had a
population of half a million. It was the heart of
Catalonia, which was the most industrialized and
modern region in Spain. Proud of this identity,
Barcelona's enterprising middle class supported
innovation of any kind, including all things cultural.
Therefore the Catalan art movement, "modernisme"
was able to spread rapidly there. This was a branch of
the Art Nouveau movement which flourished from the
1890s throughout western Europe and the USA. It was
an elegant, decorative style of art. Barcelona was able
to boast that it had the internationally famous architect
Antonio Gaudí, who designed the church of the
Sagrada Familia in the city. His style was influenced
partly by the rise of modernisme, and people in
cultured circles discussed the buildings he created
with great interest. So, in Barcelona, Picasso found a
stimulating atmosphere where a close eye was kept on
what was happening abroad, especially on any new
trends in art.

♦ HERMENEGILDO
ANGLADA CAMARASA
Pablo Picasso, 1900,
pen and gouache on
paper, 9.6 x 10.7 cm
(3²/₃ x 4¹/₃ in)
(Picasso Museum,
Barcelona).

♦ RAMÓN PICHOT
Pablo Picasso, 1900,
pen and watercolor
on paper, 8.8 x 8.9 cm
(3¹/₂ x 3¹/₂ in)
(Metropolitan
Museum of Art,
New York).

♦ THE MENU
Pablo Picasso, 1899-
1900, 21.8 x 16.4 cm
(8¹/₂ x 6¹/₂ in)
(Picasso Museum,
Barcelona).

♦ LA LONJA
The School of Fine
Arts was on the second
floor of the Stock
Exchange building.

ELS QUATRE GATS ♦
On 12 June 1897 "Els
Quatre Gats" ("The
Four Cats") opened
in Barcelona. It was
café, night-club, beer-
house and restaurant
and became a
meeting place for the
city's artists and
writers.

JAUME SABARTÈS ♦
He liked the works
exhibited at the café
and was already
convinced that
Picasso was a great
artist.

PABLO PICASSO ♦
He could not afford to
buy frames, so he
fixed his works to the
wall with thumb
tacks.

2. PICASSO'S LIFE ♦ *In autumn 1895, José Ruiz moved
his family to Barcelona, where he had been appointed to
teach at the School of Fine Arts called La Lonja.
Although only thirteen, younger than the age required
for entrance, Pablo was able to attend the school because
of his brilliant performance in the entrance exam. Two
years later, helped by his wealthy uncle, Salvador, he
went to Madrid to study at the prestigious Royal
Academy of San Fernando. He passed the entrance exam
with ease, but was soon disappointed with the teaching
methods and began to neglect his lessons, preferring to
visit the Prado, to view the works of art there. After a
bout of scarlet fever, he convalesced at Horta de Ebro
with a friend, Manuel Pallarès. When he returned to
Barcelona in 1899, he was more mature. He was ready
to plunge into the city's active cultural life and became
part of a group of artists who met at a café called
"Els Quatre Gats" ("The Four Cats").* ➻

♦ LOLA RUIZ PICASSO
Pablo Picasso, 1900, charcoal and water-color on paper, 48 x 32 cm (19 x 12½ in) (Picasso Museum, Barcelona).

♦ JOAN VIDAL VENTOSA
Pablo Picasso, 1900, charcoal and colored crayons on paper, 47 x 27 cm (18½ x 10⅔ in) (Picasso Museum, Barcelona).

♦ SABARTÈS PORTRAIT
Pablo Picasso, 1900, charcoal and water-color on paper, 48 x 32 cm (19 x 12½ in) (Picasso Museum, Barcelona).

♦ SABARTÈS SEATED
Pablo Picasso, 1900, charcoal and water-color on paper, 50.5 x 33 cm (20 x 13 in) (Picasso Museum, Barcelona).

♦ SEBASTIÁ JUNYER-VIDAL
Pablo Picasso, 1900, pencil, colored crayon and watercolor, 21 x 16 cm (8⅓ x 6⅓ in) (Picasso Museum, Barcelona).

♦ RAMÓN REVENTOS
Pablo Picasso, 1900, charcoal, conté crayon and water-color on paper, 66.5 x 30.1 cm (26 x 12 in) (Picasso Museum, Barcelona).

♦ PICTURES
The walls at Els Quatre Gats were covered with paintings, reproductions and drawings. The most eye-catching was a panel painted by Ramón Casas, of a tandem ridden by himself and Pere Romeu, the proprietor of the café.

♦ RAMÓN CASAS
This well-known portrait painter showed an interest in the work of the very young Pablo.

♦ AN EXHIBITION AT ELS QUATRE GATS
Poetry readings, shows and occasional exhibitions were organized at the café. On 1 February 1900 an exhibition of Picasso's work opened there. It included portraits of regular customers as well as pictures of Pablo's closest friends who belonged to his "tertulia", a Spanish word for a regular group of friends who meet daily to talk and joke in a café. Although mounted at minimum cost, the exhibition rivaled that of Ramón Casas which had been held in the luxurious Peres salon during the previous October and at which portraits of members of Barcelona high society had been on view.

PARIS

During the early twentieth century, Paris was the world's center of modern art. Picasso's first trip to the capital was in 1900, coinciding with the opening there of the International Exhibition, a show on a greater scale than anything he had ever experienced. The city seemed to pulsate with energy and activity, with billboards everywhere and colorful and crowded streets. It had a great attraction for foreign artists who saw it as a symbol of the modern spirit. Proof of the city's importance as a center of art in 1900 was the number of places showing recognized masterpieces or new works. The treasures in the Louvre were on view. There were exhibitions at the Grand and Petit Palais. Works by David, Delacroix and the Impressionists were included in a retrospective exhibition of French painting at the Champ de Mars. And a number of private art galleries were open, such as those of Durand-Ruel and Vollard. The Salon des Artistes and the Société Nationale des Beaux-Arts were exhibiting conventional painting, and the Salon des Indépendants showed works by painters who later came to be seen as great masters: Munch, Bonnard and Van Gogh.

♦ **LODGINGS IN PARIS** Picasso and Casagemas put a deposit on an apartment in Montparnasse. But, on their first evening in Paris, persuaded that Montmartre was the better place to be, they moved into Isidro Nonell's studio at 49 rue Gabrielle in the Catalan quarter.

LA GARE D'ORSAY ♦ In the early 1870s, the Orsay Palace which housed the State Audit Court and the Council of State was destroyed by fire. The railway station, La Gare d'Orsay, was built in its place and had only just been opened when Picasso and Casagemas arrived in Paris.

3. PICASSO'S LIFE ♦ *In 1900, having decided to look for new experiences, Picasso and Carlos Casagemas took the train to Paris. Exploring the city was a great adventure. However, Picasso kept his promise to return home for the Christmas holiday. After a brief period in Madrid, where he worked as an illustrator for a new magazine,* Arte Joven, *he once more found lodgings in the Montmartre district of Paris. Here he lived in poverty, but painted a large number of works. His first Paris exhibition, at the gallery of Ambroise Vollard, earned him some notoriety and marked the beginning of his friendship with the poet Max Jacob. Early in 1902 he returned to Barcelona, but found that he could not resist the fascination of Paris. Towards the end of that year he went back for the third time. Utterly poverty-stricken, he shared a one-bedded room with Jacob. He slept during the day while Jacob was out at work; then painted at night while Jacob slept.* ≫→

♦ THE LOUVRE
Picasso went often to the Louvre and other great museums to study the works of past masters.

TROCADÉRO ♦
In this museum, Picasso was struck by his first sight of African masks and statuettes.

♦ THE CABARET DES QUAT'Z'ARTS
This was one of the cafés used by Picasso during his first stay in Paris (Bibliothèque Nationale, Paris).

THE MOULIN ♦ DE LA GALETTE
The entrance to the famous dance-hall in 1898 (Bibliothèque Nationale, Paris).

THE FIRST DEALER ♦
Pablo Picasso, *Portrait of Pedro Mañach*, 1901, oil on canvas, 100.5 x 67.5 cm (39 1/2 x 26 1/2 in) (National Gallery of Art, Washington). Mañach, the son of a wealthy Barcelona businessman, was the first art dealer to back Pablo Picasso's talent.

♦ PICASSO'S GROUP
Throughout his life, Picasso always surrounded himself with friends, building up a close network of artists and poets who supported and inspired each other. During his first visits to Paris, those he met were mostly members of the large Catalan community, including Casas, Utrillo, Sabartès, Pallarès and Paco Durrio. Driven by his extraordinary vitality, he would walk across the city from north to south, paint in his characteristically industrious way, and spend the night wandering around Montmartre and Montparnasse and in the Latin quarter. These excursions would bring him finally to the Moulin de la Galette, a traditional meeting place for Catalan emigrants, or perhaps to Zut, a squalid café with an earth floor but with walls decorated by Picasso and Pichot. The people at these cafés gave Picasso many ideas and starting-points for his paintings in this early period in Paris.

♦ ARRIVAL
When Picasso and Casagemas first arrived in Paris in 1900, the Gare d'Orsay, with its futuristic metal structure and conveyor belt for luggage, must have impressed them as the most sparklingly modern thing they had ever seen. The moment they left the train they realized that they were in a great capital.

THE BLUE PERIOD

For three years from 1901 Picasso painted works that were dominated by shades of blue. His subject-matter was the miserable lives of people shunned by society: the poor, the sick and those who had been forced to beg in order to survive. Wizened alcoholics, prostitutes and old men spending their days in squalid bars are seen in a cold, perhaps nocturnal light. Their state of deep melancholy turns them into symbols of the human condition.

♦ **THE "BATEAU LAVOIR"**
13 rue Ravignan reminded Max Jacob of a laundry boat

("bateau lavoir") on the Seine. It housed painters, sculptors, scholars and actors.

♦ **PRECEDENTS**
Artists in established styles, like Giovanni Boldini (Ferrara, 1842 - Paris, 1931), still provided fashionable Parisian society with polished, undisturbing portraits of elegant ladies and prosperous gentlemen. However, more innovative artists, influenced by the literary theories of naturalist novelists such as Emile Zola, were also beginning to paint scenes of everyday life and people from more humble backgrounds. In his painting *Absinthe*, above, 1876, oil on canvas, 92 x 68 cm (36¼ x 26¾ in) (Musée d'Orsay, Paris), the French painter Edgar Degas was not afraid of representing alcoholism, which was widespread among the working class.
The Norwegian Edvard Munch (Löten, 1863 - Ekely, 1944) used dark colors to create a dimly lit atmosphere in *Girl Washing*, below, 1896, oil on wood, 74.5 x 59 cm (29⅓ x 23¼ in) (Nasjonalgalleriet, Oslo). The painting communicates a deeply sorrowful state of mind.

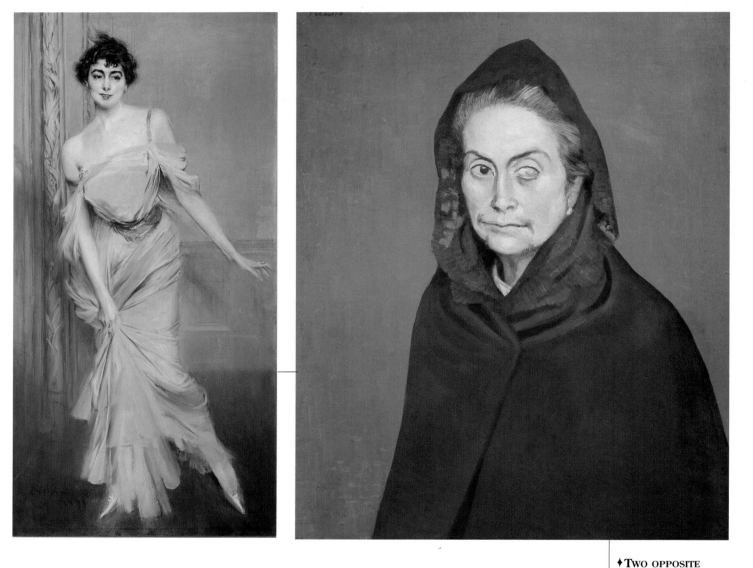

4. PICASSO'S LIFE ♦ *Life was hard for Picasso and Jacob in their lodgings on boulevard Voltaire. Both suffered from hunger and cold and no-one bought any of the Blue Period paintings. Discouraged, Picasso went back to his family in Barcelona. He painted in the studio which he had shared with Casagemas and was glad to renew contact with his friends from Els Quatre Gats, like Pallarès and Sabartès. Nonetheless, in 1904, he returned to Paris for good. A crumbling building inhabited by penniless artists, which Jacob called the "Bateau Lavoir" (laundry boat), became his home for five years. He worked at night by the light of an oil-lamp and slept by day among piles of canvas and a jumble of paints. He also found the time to join Spanish friends at the "Lapin Agile" tavern, the meeting place of avant-gardists such as Braque and Apollinaire.* ➤

♦ **AT THE RAT MORT**
Henri de Toulouse-Lautrec, 1899-1900, oil on canvas, 55 x 45 cm (21⅔ x 17⅔ in) (Courtauld Institute Galleries, London).

♦ **TWO OPPOSITE WORLDS**
Above left: *Portrait of Mrs Charles Max* by Giovanni Boldini, 1896, oil on canvas, 200 x 100 cm (78¾ x 39⅓ in) (Musée d'Orsay, Paris). Compare the showy elegance of this portrait with the poverty and sickness of Pablo Picasso's *Celestina*, above, 1904, oil on canvas, 81 x 60 cm (32 x 23⅔ in) (Picasso Museum, Paris).

♦ **DIFFERENT CHOICES**
Henri Matisse was a master at using contrasting colors to create warmth and brightness, as in *Portrait with Green Line*, left, 1905, oil on canvas, 46 x 55 cm (18 x 21²/₃ in) (Staatens Museum for Kunst, Copenhagen). Picasso used blue for the whole of the figure in *Self-portrait with Overcoat*, right, 1901, oil on canvas, 81 x 60 cm (32 x 23²/₃ in) (Picasso Museum, Paris), to convey a feeling of hopelessness and depression.

1

2

♦ **PICASSO AND THE FAUVES**
The bright, non-naturalistic color and touch of irony seen in the detail from the *Portrait of Kahnweiler*, 1907, by Kees van Dongen (1), oil on canvas, 65 x 54 cm (25¹/₂ x 21¹/₄ in) (Oscar Ghez Modern Art Foundation, Geneva), are characteristics of the Fauve style of painting. Picasso took a different course. With the use of just one color in his *Man in Blue* (2), 1903, oil on canvas, 90 x 78 cm (35¹/₂ x 30³/₄ in) (Picasso Museum, Paris), he conveyed a sense of deep feeling. *Woman in a Chemise* by André Derain (detail, 3), 1906, oil on canvas, 100 x 81 cm (39¹/₃ x 32 in) (Staatens Museum for Kunst, Copenhagen), expresses vital energy. By contrast, Picasso's *Mother and Child* (4), 1902, oil on canvas, 40.5 x 33 cm (16 x 13 in) (Scottish National Gallery of Modern Art, Edinburgh), gives a sense of sorrowful isolation.

3

4

LA VIE

Suffering and failure seem to weigh down on the two pairs of figures who are placed so that they confront one another in this painting entitled *La Vie* – "Life". Two lovers are shown on the left, the woman leaning on the man's shoulder and staring away towards the floor. The man points, with his hand lowered, at a pinched-looking woman who is holding a sleeping baby. The space between the figures is filled with two paintings against a wall.

♦ **THE WORK**
La Vie, 1903, oil on canvas, 196.5 x 128.5 cm (77 x 50¹/₂ in) (Cleveland Museum of Art, Cleveland, Ohio). This is one of the most important paintings of the Blue Period, bringing together all Picasso's concerns and ideas from this stage of his life. Unlike other Blue Period works, which had been ignored, *La Vie* was an immediate commercial success. Picasso painted it in Barcelona in May 1903, and it was bought at the beginning of June, within days of his finishing it, by the Parisian collector Jean Saint-Gaudens. In art-conscious Barcelona this event was deemed worthy of an article in the newspaper *Liberal* on 4 June 1903.

Top: study for *La Vie*, 1903, pencil on paper, 14.5 x 9.5 cm (5³/₄ x 3³/₄ in) (Picasso Museum, Barcelona).

Below: study for *La Vie*, 1903, pen and Indian ink on paper, 15.9 x 11 cm (6¹/₄ x 4¹/₃ in) (Picasso Museum, Paris).

PREPARATORY ♦ DRAWING
Pablo Picasso, *Man and Pregnant Woman*, 1903, pencil on paper, 23 x 17.8 cm (9 x 7 in) (Picasso Museum, Barcelona). The woman's pose here is very similar to that of the younger woman in *La Vie*.

♦ **THE LOVERS' POSE**
Pablo Picasso, *The Embrace*, 1903, crayon on paper, 98 x 57 cm (38¹/₂ x 22¹/₂ in) (Orangerie, Paris). There is a feeling of pain and sorrow even in their intimacy.

The presence of the two painted canvases, in the center of the scene, suggests that the action takes place in an artist's studio. This means that we can see the lovers and the mother and child either as real people who suffer or as artist's models. The message of the painting seems to be that even the supreme human experiences – sexual love and parenthood – are sorrowful. But Picasso reminds us that they are also the sources of art, and perhaps we can draw consolation from that.

THE STUDIO ♦
Inside the Artist's Studio, 1902, pen on paper, 15 x 12.2 cm (6 x 4³/₄ in) (Picasso Museum, Barcelona).

♦ THE TWO PAINTINGS
Two paintings on a wall appear in the center background of *La Vie*. The upper one is a picture of a man and woman seated and embracing; it conveys a sense of silent suffering. The top right corner is cut diagonally. The lower painting shows a person crouching on the ground, head on knees; it symbolizes solitude.

A MODEL ♦
El Greco, *Apocalyptic Vision*, 1608-1614, oil on canvas, 225 x 193 cm (88$\frac{1}{2}$ x 76 in) (Metropolitan Museum of Art, New York). Picasso was very taken with the elongated figures of the Spanish artist El Greco.

♦ VULNERABILITY
Edvard Munch, *Adolescence*, 1894, oil on canvas, 151 x 110 cm (59$\frac{1}{2}$ x 43$\frac{1}{3}$ in) (Nasjonalgalleriet, Oslo). The girl's nakedness in this painting suggests vulnerability. The same applies to that of the two lovers in *La Vie*.

♦ CASAGEMAS
Originally it was to be a self-portrait, but gradually Picasso changed the appearance of the man in the painting (right) to look like Carlos Casagemas. This was his friend who had committed suicide in Paris in 1901 because of a failed love affair.
Left: *The Death of Casagemas*, 1901, oil on wood, 27 x 35 cm (10$\frac{2}{3}$ x 13$\frac{3}{4}$ in) (Picasso Museum, Paris).

THE ROSE PERIOD

In his Rose Period, 1905-1906, Picasso painted pictures where light and various tones of pink are dominant. Figures are drawn with delicate lines, and the whole atmosphere is less serious than in the Blue Period. At this time, Picasso found the subjects for his paintings at the circus, with its young acrobats and slender clowns. He used the world of circus performers to convey the freedom and the isolation of the artist, his own feeling of being one of a chosen group of creative outsiders. His canvases are filled with portraits of dreamy-looking women seemingly living in a dimension that is cut off from the rest of the world; or clear-featured tramps giving off a feeling of inner strength; or young people crossing broad open spaces with a horse or a dog. The physical skill of jugglers, admired by the artist during many evenings spent at the Medrano Circus, is captured in his paintings in a way that expresses the inner peace resulting from a new-found faith in the future.

♦ THE WHITE CLOWN AND AUGUSTE
The first equestrian circus was founded in 1770 by Philip Astley, near Westminster, London. Jugglers and brilliant trick riders were the main performers. As time went by, other acts were added. Clowns were comedians, mime artists, acrobats and musicians all at the same time. The clown dressed in white with a painted face played a despot-like character, overbearing and cold-hearted. He was often a good musician. To counter-balance him there was the figure of Auguste, good-natured and down on his luck, dressed in baggy clothes and over-sized shoes. The Auguste was first played in 1864 by Tom Bellig, a ring-master with an English circus. At the beginning of the twentieth century, the Medrano Circus of Paris presented Antonet as the white clown and Adrian Wellach (below) as Auguste, said to be the greatest of all times. Wellach (1880-1959), also known as Grock, was a good friend of Picasso.
Top: a poster from 1912.

♦ NINETEENTH-CENTURY CIRCUSES
Equestrian circuses began to be very successful from 1850 onwards. There were great traveling circuses with their big tops, and also some important permanent ones. One of the best-known of these was the Medrano Circus in Paris.

THE MEDRANO ♦ CIRCUS
The building in Paris where the Medrano Circus gave its performances was in Montmartre, not far from the Bateau Lavoir where Picasso lived and had his studio.

♦ DEGAS' ACROBAT
Edgar Degas, *Miss Lala at the Fernando Circus*, 1879, oil on canvas, 117 x 77 cm (46 x 30⅓ in) (National Gallery, London).

PORTRAIT OF ✦ A WOMAN
Pablo Picasso, *Seated Nude*, 1905, oil on cardboard on board, 106 x 76 cm (41¾ x 30 in) (Georges Pompidou Center, Paris). A warm, yellow-pink light falls on the woman's body.

THE ACROBAT'S ✦ FAMILY
Pablo Picasso, *The Acrobat's Family with a Monkey*, 1905, gouache, watercolor, crayon and Indian ink on cardboard, 104 x 75 cm (41 x 29½ in) (Konstmuseum, Göteborg). The monkey introduces an element of surprise and gives the painting symbolic weight.

5. PICASSO'S LIFE ✦ *Returning home during a storm, Picasso met Fernande Olivier in the hallway of the Bateau Lavoir where she was sheltering from the rain. The few light-hearted words they exchanged were enough to form a friendship which developed into an important love affair. Fernande remained the artist's companion until 1912. She was his favorite model and the first to set eyes on a great many of his masterpieces. When he was not shut away in his studio painting, Picasso derived great enjoyment from going to the Medrano Circus along with his artist and writer friends. In 1905 he met Leo and Gertrude Stein, who rescued him from poverty by drawing him into a circle of art lovers willing to buy his works. They included the extremely wealthy Russian collector Sergei Shchukin and the German Wilhelm Uhde. The Steins were valuable support for a painter who, unlike Matisse, refused to exhibit in the official salons.* ➤

THE FAMILY OF SALTIMBANQUES

A group of six figures is placed in a desolate, desert-like landscape. The people are arranged in a descending diagonal. In the left-hand and central areas of the painting are the circus performers, including a girl holding a basket of flowers. On the far right, a solitary young woman is seated. The effect of spreading out the subjects in this way is to highlight the character of each individual.

♦ SKETCH
A sketch by Picasso for *The Family of Saltimbanques*, 1905, pencil and charcoal, 37.4 x 26.9 cm (14³/₄ x 10¹/₂ in) (Picasso Museum, Paris).

♦ THE WORK
The Family of Saltimbanques, 1905, oil on canvas, 212.8 x 229.6 cm (83³/₄ x 90¹/₃ in) (National Gallery of Art, Washington). A detail is shown below. Seemingly painted all at once, and considered the masterpiece of Picasso's Rose Period, this work was in fact the result of a difficult process during which many changes were made. X-ray examination reveals several earlier versions behind the final painting. Picasso began the work in 1904 and at first it included a larger number of figures which he then reduced to two. Still unsatisfied, he returned to the idea of a group. The background and the position of each of the figures were also slowly changed until the work was finally completed during the summer of 1905.

♦ A MODEL
Edouard Manet, *The Old Musician*, 1862, oil on canvas, 187.4 x 248.3 cm (73³/₄ x 97³/₄ in) (National Gallery of Art, Washington).

Harlequin, the acrobat and the jester are circus performers, chosen by Picasso to symbolize his feelings about the artist's condition. In French, "Saltimbanques" are buffoons, and Picasso probably used this rather derogatory term in self-mockery, seeing that it applied, in a sense, to all artists. Dropped in an unreal landscape, the performers communicate a mysterious feeling of solitude. They are sad, but also proud of their talent which makes them unique.

♦ STUDY
Pablo Picasso, *Tio Pepe and the Family of Saltimbanques*, 1905, pen, watercolor and charcoal on paper, 20.2 x 31.2 cm (8 x 12¹/₄ in) (Picasso Museum, Paris).

Primitivism

At the turn of the twentieth century, many artists including Picasso, Gauguin and Matisse took an interest in objects from ancient or distant cultures. African tribal masks, wooden or stone figures from Asia and Oceania, Egyptian statues and ancient sculpture became important sources of inspiration. The modern artists were excited by the expressiveness and primitive energy of these objects and sought to convey such qualities in their own figurative art.

✦ FANG MASK
Gabon, painted wood (National Museum of Modern Art, Paris).

✦ COLLECTORS
As a result of scientific and archeological expeditions, many objects from ancient Mediterranean cultures and countries outside Europe were on show at the 1867 International Exhibition in Paris. At the same time, the circulation of magazines specializing in these kinds of curiosities also became much broader. Wealthy middle-class Parisians began to collect ancient Egyptian artefacts and Asian and Japanese art.
In the early twentieth century, African masks and carvings became a fashion craze. Artists were able to study them for fresh inspiration.

✦ IDOL
Paul Gauguin, *Oviri*, 1894, earthenware, height 75 cm (29½ in) (Musée d'Orsay, Paris). This piece portrays an exotic god representing the powers of love and death.

✦ THE LIBYAN CHIEF BACHASOU
Bronze (Louvre, Paris).

6. PICASSO'S LIFE ✦ *In March 1906 the Steins introduced Picasso to Henri Matisse. The two artists exchanged views on each other's work, and this was the start of a friendship which would last for years, despite great professional rivalry between the two men. Vollard had bought almost all the canvases painted during the Rose Period for the sum of two thousand francs, and so Picasso suddenly had some financial stability. He and Fernande decided to travel to Spain, to see his family and also to take some time off in Gosol, a village in the Pyrenees. The solitude and the countryside had a positive effect on Picasso, who worked on a series of portraits marking the beginning of his "primitive" phase. In August 1906, when a typhoid epidemic broke out in Gosol, Picasso and Fernande returned to Paris. ➤*

✦ INSPIRED BY AFRICAN SCULPTURE
Above left: Henri Matisse, *Standing Nude*, 1906, oil on canvas, 92 x 64 cm (36¼ x 25¼ in) (Tate Gallery, London).
Above: Pablo Picasso, *Two Female Nudes*, 1906, oil on canvas, 151.3 x 93 cm (59½ x 36½ in) (Museum of Modern Art, New York).

✦ A MODEL
Woman Bearing Offerings, Egyptian, 11th Dynasty (Cairo Museum).

♦ **PICASSO'S COLLECTION**
At the beginning of the twentieth century, the most notable dealers in primitive art in Paris were Emile Hayman and Joseph Brummer. They never went to Africa, but selected the best pieces brought back by travelers, missionaries and agents whom they had paid to buy on their behalf. Picasso bought many carvings from Africa and Oceania and built up a large collection over the years.

♦ **PRE-COLUMBIAN SCULPTURE**
Paul Gauguin, *La Belle Angèle*, 1889, oil on canvas, 92 x 73 cm (36¼ x 28¾ in) (Musée d'Orsay, Paris). On the left is a pre-Columbian sculpture.

EGYPTIAN STATUES ♦
Edgar Degas, *Portrait of Hélène Rouart*, 1886, oil on canvas, 162 x 123 cm (63¾ x 48½ in) (National Gallery, London). Next to the painting's main subject, the artist placed three Egyptian statuettes, showing them considerably larger than their actual size. This was meant as a reference to the work of Hélène's father, Henri Rouart, a collector and friend of Degas.

ANCIENT SPANISH ♦
SCULPTURE
Man Attacked by a Lion, detail of a bas relief found in Osuna, late VI-III centuries BC, height 41 cm (16¼ in) (Museo Arqueológico Nacional, Madrid). Picasso was able to study works like this which were put on exhibition at the Louvre from September 1904.

♦ **AFRICAN INFLUENCE**
Pablo Picasso, *Portrait of Gertrude Stein*, detail, 1906, oil on canvas, 99.6 x 81.3 cm (39¼ x 32 in) (Metropolitan Museum of Art, New York). The face is like a carved wooden mask.

THE STEINS

Many art collectors who bought non-traditional contemporary works at the beginning of the twentieth century also decorated their homes with objects in a range of styles and from various ages. Always in search of fresh aesthetic experiences, these wealthy people – who were sometimes also avant-garde intellectuals like the Steins – acquired African carvings, Japanese prints and other exotic objets d'art, as well as the daring works of modern art which often owed a good deal to them. This type of collecting was practiced by a still very limited number of connoisseurs, who were excited by the idea of discovering unknown artists and helping them to gain recognition. Members of the Stein family, especially Gertrude, Leo and Michael, played a fundamental part in finding, collecting and promoting the work of many now famous twentieth-century artists.

♦ THE STEIN FAMILY
There were five brothers and sisters in the Stein family. Michael, the oldest, was born in 1865. Simon and Bertha were not interested in art. Leo was born in 1872 and Gertrude in 1874. They were Americans, of German origin. Their father, Daniel Stein, made his fortune in the clothing business and later occupied himself with railways, mines and the stock market. When the children were young, the family moved around a great deal, making many trips from the United States to Europe. After their parents died, the five brothers and sisters went their separate ways, but met up again at the beginning of the twentieth century when Leo, Gertrude, Michael and Michael's wife Sarah settled in Paris. Top: Gertrude Stein.

GERTRUDE STEIN ♦
Gertrude Stein became a celebrated – or notorious – experimental writer, as well as a generous friend and patron of artists such as Matisse and Picasso and, later, writers like Ernest Hemingway. She lived with her brother, Leo, at 27 rue de Fleurus, and on Saturday evenings held receptions, at which the guests were famous people from the Parisian art and literary world.

KAHNWEILER ♦
The art dealer whom Picasso liked the most was the gallery owner Daniel-Henri Kahnweiler. He was one of the first to appreciate and champion the Cubist style of painting.

♦ Pablo Picasso

♦ Pablo Picasso   ♦ Pablo Picasso

Félix-Edouard Vallotton ♦

Pablo Picasso ♦

Henri Matisse ♦

♦ **VOLLARD**
This astute and eccentric dealer, who handled the work of artists like Cézanne and Matisse, owned a gallery that looked more like a second-hand shop. He was often gruff with his clients and refused to sell them the paintings they wanted.

♦ **1914-1920: A MOBILE COLLECTION**
Each year the Steins changed around the positions of the works hanging on their studio walls, to give pride of place to their latest favorite.

♦ Henri Matisse   ♦ Pablo Picasso   ♦ Pablo Picasso

♦ Pablo Picasso

♦ Paul Cézanne

♦ **LEO STEIN**
When he was young, Leo studied ancient art, philosophy and biology, never applying himself for long to any one of these subjects, as his enthusiasm for them waxed and waned. On the advice of the art historian, Bernard Berenson, in 1903 he went to the Vollard gallery and began to acquire works by Cézanne. Two years later, he bought a work by Picasso, from the dealer Sagot. It was the first of many Picasso paintings that he would buy.

CUBISM

Cubism is generally considered to have been the most revolutionary development in painting in the twentieth century. With it was born a truly modern form of artistic expression, which broke away completely from styles of the past by creating a new way of representing reality. Cubism cast aside the use of linear perspective, which had been established by Renaissance artists. Instead of showing a three-dimensional object as we see it in real life, from one particular angle, Cubist painting showed it from all points of view at once, on a two-dimensional surface. The combination of the various views resulted in a fragmented image, and complex and fascinating geometric patterns were thus created. Picasso's work *Les Demoiselles d'Avignon* (page 26) of 1907 was one of the earliest examples of Cubism. Between that year and 1914, Picasso and the French painter Georges Braque explored and developed Cubist ideas. Among their sources of inspiration were the later paintings of Paul Cézanne and Iberian and African sculpture.

♦THE HUMAN BODY
The human body, redesigned by Picasso's Cubism, consists of a set of angular planes. Its rigidity makes it look as if it has been carved in wood or stone. Figures by the Italian Giovanni Bracelli seem to anticipate this style. Above is a detail from an illustration in Bracelli's collection, *Bizzarrie* (Florence, 1644).

Compare Bracelli's drawing and Picasso's *Nude Woman Geometrized in Pose* (above), 1908, charcoal on paper, 62.7 x 48.1 cm (24²/₃ x 19 in) (Picasso Museum, Paris).

♦TOWARDS CUBISM
Paul Cézanne, *Mont Sainte-Victoire*, c.1887, oil on canvas, 67 x 92 cm (26¹/₃ x 36¹/₄ in) (Courtauld Institute Galleries, London). Cézanne is considered the inspirational master of Cubist painters, the first to have created a new visual language by his manipulation of space, volume and color.

♦HOUSES ON A HILL
Pablo Picasso, 1909, oil on canvas, 65 x 81 cm (25¹/₂ x 32 in) (Museum of Modern Art, New York). Picasso has interpreted the houses and rooftops in the little town of Horta de Ebro as an arrangement of stylized solid shapes. The perspective has been substantially changed and the buildings have been transformed into a cluster of crystals.

♦IBERIAN SCULPTURE
Madonna and Child, twelfth century, polychrome wood, height 77 cm (30¹/₃ in) (Museu d'Art de Catalunya, Barcelona). Picasso's early Cubist paintings show that he had been influenced by the style of this sculpture, which he saw during his stay in Gosol in 1906.

♦PAOLO UCCELLO
The Battle of San Romano, Unseating of Bernardino della Ciarda, 1456, 182 x 323 cm (71²/₃ x 127 in) (Uffizi, Florence). Paolo Uccello closely studied the technique of linear perspective. Cubism broke away from such traditional perspective. Nonetheless, the works of both Uccello and Picasso are the result of meticulous research into how to show volume in space.

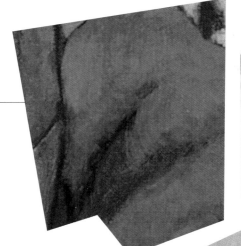

✦ GEORGES BRAQUE
Picasso and Braque were very close friends during the Cubism years. Together they proceeded to revolutionize the rules of painting. Their paths divided when the First World War broke out and Braque was called to serve in the army while Picasso stayed in Paris. After the war, Braque's style became less angular. In 1961 he was the first living artist to have his work exhibited at the Louvre.

✦ BRAQUE'S CUBISM
Georges Braque, *Houses at Estaque*, 1908, oil on canvas, 73 x 59.5 cm (28³⁄₄ x 23¹⁄₂ in) (Kunstmuseum, Bern). Braque's application of color in his Cubist paintings was particularly subtle. Here, line and geometry create a very solid effect.

✦ THE USE OF THE OVAL SHAPE
Pablo Picasso, *Violin, Glass, Pipe and Ink-pot*, 1912, oil on canvas, 81 x 54 cm (32 x 21¹⁄₄ in) (Narodni Galerie, Prague). The Cubist method of dividing up space created a new, segmented view with many right angles. The oval shape of the canvas has the effect of strengthening these angles, making them more noticeable in contrast to the curves of the space containing them. The inclusion of printed letters links the painting to the real world outside, with its billboards and newspapers.

7. PICASSO'S LIFE ✦ *Picasso visited an exhibition of African sculpture at the Trocadéro ethnological museum in July 1907. It made a strong impression on him, contributing to the development of his new ideas about painting. Meanwhile, his circle of friends was growing. He began a working relationship with the art dealer, Daniel-Henri Kahnweiler; he organized a party at the Bateau Lavoir in honor of the painter Henri Rousseau; and he met Georges Braque, a Norman, who joined him in his researches leading to Cubism. In September 1909, Picasso and Fernande moved into a large, luxury apartment on boulevard Clichy. Picasso's fame increased abroad too, especially in Germany and the USA. He now led a more comfortable life, but his relationship with Fernande was under strain and in 1912 they broke up.* ➤➔

LES DEMOISELLES D'AVIGNON

The figures of five naked women fill the canvas and are arranged following a diagonal line which starts from the hand, top left, and finishes with the crouching body, bottom right. The treatment of the figures (especially the heads) emphasizes the fact that the painting consists of three vertical sections corresponding to the woman standing on the left, the two women face on, and the two on the right.

♦ **THE WORK**
Les Demoiselles d'Avignon, 1907, oil on canvas, 243.9 x 233.7 cm (96 x 92 in) (Museum of Modern Art, New York). The first preparatory sketches for the painting date back to autumn 1906. The planning stage then continued until May 1907, with Picasso doing over 800 drawings. The work was finally painted during the following two months. For many years it was considered scandalous and incomprehensible and was long hidden away in Picasso's private collection.

♦ **PREPARATORY STUDIES**
Three studies for *Les Demoiselles d'Avignon*. Top: *Woman's Head*, 1906-1907, pencil on paper, 63.5 x 48 cm (25 x 19 in). Center: *The Sailor*, pencil on paper, 22.4 x 17.5 cm (8¾ x 6¾ in). Below: *Study*, 1907, charcoal on paper, 8.7 x 9 cm (3¼ x 3½ in). (Picasso Museum, Paris).

NUDE WOMAN ♦ STANDING
Pablo Picasso, 1907, carved and painted wood, 31.8 x 8.3 cm (12½ x 3¼ in) (Picasso Museum, Paris). A sculpture obviously inspired by African art.

This revolutionary painting signaled the beginning of Cubism. In it, Picasso re-worked various ideas suggested by African, ancient Iberian and Egyptian art. The distortion of the human figures and the space surrounding them was unprecedented. All the elements are portrayed not as they are seen in reality but as a combination of angular, flat shapes. Picasso was all the more daring in tackling in this way a hallowed subject of European art: the nude.

♦ **A DRAFT**
Bust of a Woman, study for *Les Demoiselles d'Avignon*, 1907, oil on canvas, 65 x 58 cm (25½ x 23 in) (Pompidou Center, Paris). The face looks like a wood carving.

MASK ✦
A detail from *Les Demoiselles d'Avignon*. This woman's face is elongated and compressed. It is seemingly based on an African mask.

✦ NON-REALISTIC
Detail from *Les Demoiselles d'Avignon*. Like the whole, the foot is not drawn realistically.

✦ AN EARLIER CONCEPTION
Pablo Picasso, a study for *Les Demoiselles d'Avignon*, 1907, pencil and crayon on paper, 47.7 x 63.5 cm (18 ³/₄ x 25 in) (Kupferstichkabinett, Öffentliche Kunstsammlung, Basel). Originally Picasso planned to include seven figures in the painting, one of them a sailor.

CÉZANNE ✦
Three Bathers by Paul Cézanne, 1879-1882, oil on canvas, 52 x 55 cm (20¹/₂ x 21²/₃ in) (Musée du Petit Palais, Paris). Picasso was influenced by Cézanne's powerful nudes.

✦ INGRES
A traditional masterpiece that influenced Picasso was *Le Bain Turc* by Jean-Auguste-Dominique Ingres, 1862, oil on canvas, 108 cm (42¹/₂ in) in diameter (Louvre, Paris).

COLLAGE

Still Life with Chair Caning, detail.

Working with Cubist ideas and developing them further, Picasso and Braque invented new techniques where they incorporated everyday materials into their paintings. The two artists made collages and papier collé pictures using newspaper, wallpaper, sheets of music and bottle labels, which were cut out, glued and mounted. Next, the collage became a three-dimensional "assemblage", an object made up of various pieces of wood, cardboard or metal arranged together in a kind of sculpture. All these techniques, for which the artists chose to use everyday or even scrap materials, represented a clear revolt against the traditional concept of what made a work of art.

♦ **DEVELOPING THE TECHNIQUE**
This photograph was taken by Picasso himself in 1913 and reveals the kind of research he carried out to turn collage into a technique closer to sculpture than to painting. He brought humor and great creativity to the task.

♦ **COLLAGE AND PAPIER COLLÉ**
A collage is made by pasting pieces of paper, fabric or other material to a surface to create an artistic composition. We know that this technique was used in Japan in the tenth century. Cubists began using it in 1912. Juan Gris used pages from books, music scores and pieces of newspaper.
The avant-garde artists of the Futurist movement (Carlo Carrà, Enrico Prampolini, Ardengo Soffici, Mario Sironi) also began making collages in 1914, but used only colored or decorative papers. The correct name for this particular kind of collage is papier collé.

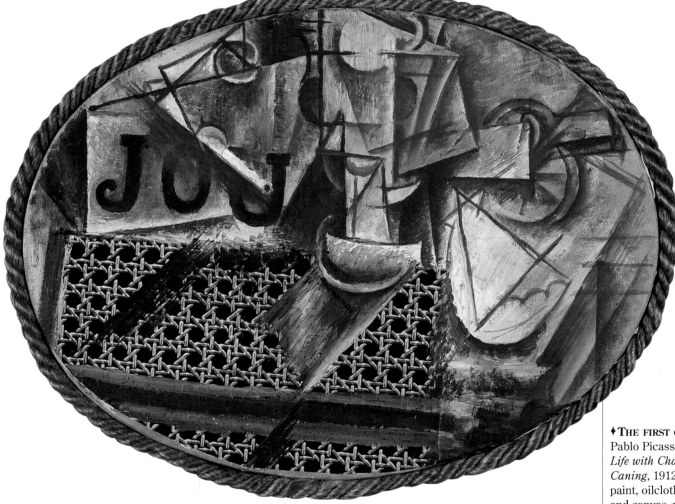

♦ **BOTTLE ON A TABLE**
Pablo Picasso, after 8 December 1912, papiers collés and charcoal on newspaper, 62 x 44 cm (24¹/₂ x 17¹/₃ in) (Picasso Museum, Paris).

8. PICASSO'S LIFE ♦ *In spring 1912, Picasso and Marcelle Humbert, the artist's new companion (whom he called "Eva"), moved into a house in the south of France, in the small, quiet town of Sorgues sur Ouvèze. They often saw Braque and his wife who lived nearby. After the summer, they returned to Paris and lodged in a house in Montparnasse, the elegant district of grand cafés like Le Dôme and La Coupole. This was one of the happiest periods in Picasso's life, but it came to an abrupt end in August 1914, with the outbreak of the First World War. Vollard and Kahnweiler closed their galleries, many of his closest friends were drafted into the army, and his beloved Eva died of tuberculosis. In these circumstances, Picasso felt vulnerable and isolated.* ➤

♦ **THE FIRST COLLAGE**
Pablo Picasso, *Still Life with Chair Caning,* 1912, oil paint, oilcloth, paper and canvas, with a rope frame, 29 x 37 cm (11¹/₂ x 14¹/₂ in) (Picasso Museum, Paris).

♦ **MUSIC IN THE COLLAGE**
Pablo Picasso, *Violin and Sheet Music,* 1912, papiers collés on cardboard, 78 x 65 cm (30³/₄ x 25¹/₂ in) (Picasso Museum, Paris). The subject of the work is made clear by the presence of the actual page of music.

♦ **ASSEMBLAGE**
Pablo Picasso, *Guitar and Bottle of Bass*, 1913, parts in wood, paper, charcoal and nails on board, 89.5 x 80 x 14 cm (35¼ x 31½ x 5½ in) (Picasso Museum, Paris). An object like this is halfway between a painting and a sculpture. It was the beginning of a new art form.

♦ **MAN WITH PIPE (THE SMOKER)**
Pablo Picasso, 1914, oil and paper on canvas, 138 x 65.5 cm (54⅓ x 25¾ in) (Picasso Museum, Paris).

♦ **PAPIERS COLLÉS**
Georges Braque, *Aria de Bach*, 1913, oil and papiers collés on canvas, 62 x 47 cm (24½ x 18½ in) (National Gallery of Art, Washington). Braque began to create papier collé pictures in summer 1912, using paper that resembled the surface of wood.

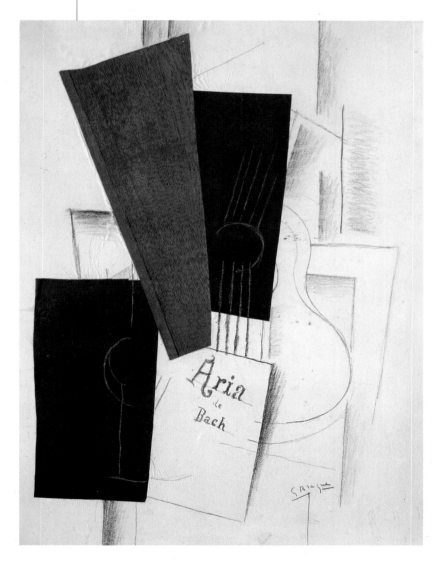

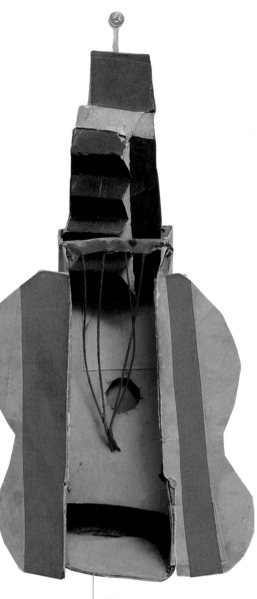

♦ **EXPERIMENT**
Pablo Picasso, *Guitar*, 1912, cardboard, paper, canvas, string and pencil, 33 x 18 x 9.5 cm (13 x 7 x 3¾ in) (Picasso Museum, Paris). Here the collage became a three-dimensional object.

♦ **LATER DEVELOPMENTS**
Picasso developed the technique of collage to create more and more complex works. By overlapping materials, he suggested connections between different spatial planes and so gave an illusion of depth. At the end of 1915 Picasso abandoned this technique which was then taken up, in various ways, by artists belonging to later art movements. One example was the Surrealist Max Ernst. Also, from the late 1940s, Henri Matisse, bedridden and unable to paint, used papiers collés for some large compositions. He claimed that "cutting into color" with scissors produced results as fine as painting.

♦ **HENRI MATISSE**
Left: *Creole Ballerina*, 1951, gouache on cut-paper glued, 205 x 120 cm (80¾ x 47¼ in) (Matisse Museum, Nice). Right: *Blue Nude II*, 1952, gouache on cut-paper, glued, 116 x 89 cm (45⅔ x 35 in) (Georges Pompidou Center, Paris).

PICASSO IN ITALY

Picasso arrived in Rome towards the end of February 1917 and remained in Italy until May of that year. It was a short stay, but long enough for the artist to experience some creative insights that would affect his work. The trip gave him the opportunity to design the scenery for the ballet *Parade*, which was to be produced by the Sergei Diaghilev company in May, at the Châtelet Theatre in Paris. Picasso's stay in Rome coincided with the beginning of a new cycle of paintings in which he abandoned Cubism for a more traditional, figurative style. No doubt, being in a city where he could admire the impressive remains of ancient Roman civilization, seeing works by Michelangelo and Raphael in the Vatican, and visiting Pompeii, Naples and Florence were experiences that guided Picasso towards a different style of art in the years immediately following. He turned to forms that were much closer to the classical tradition.

♦ **THE REASON FOR GOING TO ITALY**
The poet Jean Cocteau suggested to Picasso that he design the sets and costumes for *Parade*, a ballet which was to be produced by the Sergei Diaghilev company, and the two of them went to meet Diaghilev, who was working in Rome. Picasso's acceptance of the work of set designer shocked his colleagues, who regarded this as a crime against the strict principles of Cubism.

The music for *Parade* was by Erik Satie and the libretto by Cocteau. With Satie's agreement, many of the ballet sequences were changed to suit Picasso's designs for Cubist costumes made up of overlapping geometric shapes and others on a circus theme. Despite its high quality, the ballet was less successful than expected.

Top: photo of Sergei Diaghilev. Center: Jean Cocteau. Bottom: Portrait of Erik Satie by Picasso, 1920, graphite and charcoal, 62 x 47.7 cm (24½ x 18¾ in) (Picasso Museum, Paris).

♦ **THE VILLA MEDICI**
In Rome Picasso stayed at the Hotel di Russia, in Via del Babbuino, but he worked on *Parade* in a studio in Via Margutta. From here he could see and paint various views of the Villa Medici.

♦ **PIAZZA DI SPAGNA**
Picasso, Cocteau and Diaghilev watched the models in the Piazza di Spagna.

MODELS ♦
When walking through Rome, Picasso often crossed the Piazza di Spagna. Here it was usual to find groups of girls in traditional costume from the town of Anticoli Corrado in the region of Lazio. They would wait to be employed as models by the painters who worked in the nearby Via Margutta. Their beauty is seen in many of the portraits of women that Picasso painted while in Rome.

9. PICASSO'S LIFE ♦ *In 1917 Picasso went to Rome, to meet Sergei Diaghilev. There, he fell in love with Olga Koklova, a ballerina in the Diaghilev company. To be near her, he later followed the Russian ballet to Madrid and Barcelona. Olga and Picasso were married in July 1918 and went to live in a large, two-story house in rue de la Boétie, in Paris, where they led a full and fashionable life. Picasso mixed with high society and was able to afford a luxurious life-style since the value of his paintings had considerably increased. He was deeply upset by the death of his friend, the writer Apollinaire in 1918. For the next two years he worked on stage sets. The birth of his first child, Paulo, at the beginning of 1921, cheered the artist enormously and for a while he led a peaceful domestic existence, with its regular rhythm of art production and summer holidays in elegant places like Dinard and Cap d'Antibes. ➣+*

THE CURTAIN ♦
Pablo Picasso, *Parade*, 1917, tempera on canvas, 10.6 x 17.25 m (34³/₄ x 56¹/₂ ft) (Georges Pompidou Center, Paris). This curtain, filled with fairytale figures, served to introduce the ballet.

♦ THE ACROBAT
Pablo Picasso, *Design for an Acrobat's Costume*, watercolor and graphite, 28 x 20.5 cm (11 x 8 in) (Picasso Museum, Paris).

ITALIAN MODELS ♦
Picasso studied the works of Italian old masters. In paintings such as *Head of a Woman* (detail, right), 1921, oil on canvas, 55 x 46 cm (21²/₃ x 18 in) (Picasso Museum, Paris), he was clearly influenced by Arnolfo di Cambio and Masaccio. Far right: detail of Masaccio's *The Distribution of Goods and the Punishment of Ananias*, 1424-1428 (Brancacci Chapel, Florence).

♦ RAPHAEL
The Expulsion of Eliodoro, detail, fresco, 1511-1514 (Vatican Museum, Rome). It is not known for sure whether Picasso went to see the frescoes by Michelangelo and Raphael in the Sistine Chapel, but he certainly would have known these works through reproductions.

♦ PICASSO'S ITALIANISM
Picasso was impressed by the paintings of Raphael and by the frescoes at Pompeii. Their influence is obvious in the positioning of the bodies in *The Race*, painted by Picasso in 1922, tempera on plywood, 32.5 x 41.1 cm (12³/₄ x 16 in) (Picasso Museum, Paris).

PIMPINELLA ♦
Pablo Picasso, *Study for Pimpinella's Costume*, gouache and graphite, 23.5 x 17 cm (9¹/₄ x 6²/₃ in) (Picasso Museum, Paris).

♦ ITALIAN COUNTRY WOMEN
Pablo Picasso, *L'Italienne*, 1918-1919, etching on zinc, 15 x 10 cm (6 x 4 in) (Picasso Museum, Paris). When in Rome, Picasso did not only study great works by old masters, but was also inspired by the models who stood around in the Piazza di Spagna, allowing local artists to produce drawings of Italian country customs.

THREE MUSICIANS

Three figures, masked and in costume, fill the entire canvas. The musicians are seated next to each other behind a table. From left to right they are: a pierrot playing a wind instrument, a harlequin with a guitar, and a monk holding a music score. There is a dog lying under the table. The group seems to be enlarged by the surrounding walls, which close in as if to compress the figures.

This is a late masterpiece of Synthetic Cubism, painted after Picasso had moved on. However, the grouping here obviously appealed to him, since he also painted another Three Musicians *which, apart from transposing the figures, closely resembles this one. The surface has been broken down into colored shapes, with no attempt to convey depth. Such a radical departure from traditional perspective results in a non-realistic, but still perfectly legible, portrayal of the visible world.*

THE MONK ♦
The face is painted like a mask. However, this time Picasso's inspiration did not come from an African object but from the flat surface of a sheet of paper.

♦THE PIERROT
The pierrot's costume is made up of irregular jigsaw-like shapes, in white and blue, fitted together.

THE DOG ♦
The shape of the dog under the table seems cut into the surface of the floor. It has no depth.

♦MUSIC
The large musical notes on the score emphasize the main subject matter of the painting.

♦A PASSION FOR MUSIC
Pablo Picasso, *Musical Instruments on a Table*, 1925, 162 x 204.5 cm (63¾ x 80½ in) (Centro de Arte Reina Sofia, Madrid). Picasso always loved traditional Spanish, popular music, such as cante hondo.

33

♦ LE CORBUSIER
(Charles-Edouard Jeanneret, 1887-1965) French architect, town planner, painter and sculptor. During his sixty years of working life he had a key influence on developments in the modern movement. He formulated a theory that it was the architect's responsibility to solve social problems. Everything from interior design to town planning should be included in an overall plan to improve people's lives.

♦ WALTER GROPIUS
(1883-1969)
German architect, designer and town planner.
In 1919 he founded the Bauhaus in Weimar. The aim of this new art institute was to bring together artists and architects to relate art and design to the new age of mass production. Some of the most important painters of the century, like Vasily Kandinsky and Paul Klee, were among its teaching staff. Gropius viewed architecture as a rational product, involving moral values, that could radically change the way people lived.

PAINTING AND ARCHITECTURE

At the end of the First World War, conditions in many parts of Europe had changed dramatically. The war had boosted industry and urban populations had increased. The working class, now more vocal and active through trade unions and political parties, expected some return for the heavy sacrifices made during the war. They demanded modern, clean factories, better housing, and pleasant areas to live in, with schools, hospitals and services. A generation of young architects responded to these new aspirations, creating the Functionalist style. Their buildings had no purely decorative features. Everything had an essential purpose. Plain walls contained large, light-giving windows. Flat roofs were used as gardens. Industrial methods of construction replaced the old building crafts. In architecture, the taste for simple shapes and the rejection of ornamental detail owed a good deal to the influence of Cubism.

♦ THE LA ROCHE HOUSE
Built by Le Corbusier in 1923, the building really consisted of two homes: on the right that of Albert Jeanneret, Le Corbusier's younger brother; and on the left that of Raoul La Roche, a wealthy collector of modern paintings.

PURISM ♦
As a young man, Le Corbusier devoted himself to painting. In 1919, using his real name Jeanneret, he and a friend, the painter Amédée Ozenfant, published their Purist manifesto.

AN OPEN SPACE ♦
The La Roche house was simple and quite ordinary from the outside. Inside, it was open-plan. The various floors were not completely separated; a system of galleries allowed the whole house to be viewed from any standpoint. The design of the house followed Cubist principles.

♦ OVERLAPPING OBJECTS
Georges Braque paid special attention in his Cubist works to the positions of objects in space, as can be seen in *The Clarinet*, 1912, oil on canvas, 91 x 64.5 cm (36 x 25⅓ in) (Peggy Guggenheim Collection, Venice).

♦ AN ARCHITECTURAL APPROACH TO PAINTING
In his Cubist work, Picasso followed strict rules for dividing the area of his paintings into basic geometric shapes. This same "rational" approach was adopted in the main trends in modern architecture.

♦ COLORS
An artist's influence is seen in the colors chosen for the walls of the La Roche house. Le Corbusier himself said: "The inside of the house should be white, but for the white to be appreciated, there must be a well-ordered variety of color." In effect, the dimly lit walls were painted blue and the walls in full light were painted red.

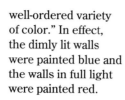

♦ A PRECURSOR
In *The Poet*, 1911, oil on canvas, 131.2 x 89.5 cm (51⅔ x 35¼ in) (Peggy Guggenheim Collection, Venice), Picasso showed objects in relation to space, in an extraordinary, illusionistic way.

♦ LIGHTING
To concentrate attention on the paintings, the gallery had almost no windows. It was illuminated by just one long, very high strip window.

♦ THE GALLERY
Le Corbusier provided a large room to house the La Roche painting collection. It was connected to the library by a long ramp. This design was later adopted for many modern art museums.

♦ THE LIBRARY
The library, a place of rest, reflection and intellectual pleasure, was the heart of the La Roche house. From here, the owner controlled his home and gallery.

♦ LA ROCHE
La Roche had asked Le Corbusier to hang his collection of Cubist paintings. The architect did much more than that. He arranged the collection and then designed a house-museum – the first example of a harmonious relationship between modern art and architecture.

AVANT-GARDE AND TRADITIONAL

In the first thirty years of the twentieth century, two contrasting movements alternately held sway in the art world. On the one hand, avant-garde trends, like Cubism and Surrealism, developed. They were revolutionary, both in their basic ideas and in the techniques that the artists adopted. On the other hand, there was a movement inspired by the theory that art should reassert the value of traditional styles and methods, and build on these. Picasso produced both avant-garde and traditional works.

♦ **GINO SEVERINI** *Motherhood*, 1916, oil on canvas, 92 x 65 cm (36¼ x 25½ in) (Museo dell'Accademia Etrusca, Cortona).

♦ **THE RETURN TO TRADITION** During the First World War, Gino Severini (1883-1966) and Carlo Carrà (1881-1966), both Italian, were among the first to return to a more classical style of painting, modeled on the old masters. Cubism was followed by a return to more traditional forms – a phenomenon described as a "return to order". This tendency was most marked in Italy and France, involving artists like Giorgio de Chirico (1888-1978) and Giorgio Morandi (1890-1964). Picasso also began to paint figures that were no longer disassembled in the Cubist style: gigantic creatures with monumental bodies, or else portraits that were almost photographic likenesses.

♦ **CARLO CARRÀ** *Yachts at the Port*, detail, 1923, oil on canvas, 64.4 x 79.9 cm (25⅓ x 31½ in) (Longhi Foundation, Florence).

♦ **TRADITIONAL STYLE** Picasso, *Self-portrait*, 1919, pencil and charcoal on paper, 64 x 49.5 cm (25 x 19½ in) (Picasso Museum, Paris).

10. PICASSO'S LIFE ♦ *Picasso had become financially very comfortable and bought himself a splendid car which, at the time, was an exceptional luxury. He lived in a beautiful house and mixed with high society. And yet he was not satisfied. His marriage to Olga was beginning to seem like a prison sentence for him. Olga had conventional ideas and was worried about outward appearances. She was also domineering, a characteristic which clashed with her husband's natural spirit of independence. Early in 1927, Picasso saw the seventeen-year-old Marie-Thérèse Walter near the Galeries Lafayette. He was struck by her beauty and spoke to her. They embarked upon a secret affair and rented an apartment quite close to where Picasso lived with Olga and Paulo.* ➤

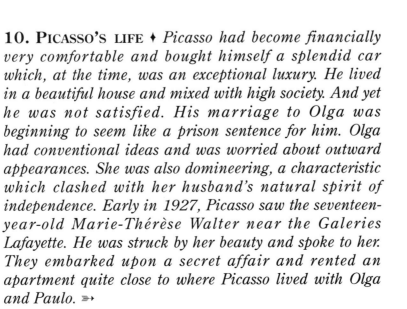

♦ **A CONTRAST** Pablo Picasso, left: *Portrait of Olga in an Armchair*, 1917, oil on canvas, 130 x 88.8 cm (51 x 35 in) (Picasso Museum, Paris); right: *Woman in an Armchair*, 1917, oil on canvas, 116 x 89.2 cm (45⅔ x 35 in) (Picasso Museum, Barcelona).

♦ **GIORGIO DE CHIRICO** *The Painter's Family*, 1926, oil on canvas, 146.4 x 114.9 cm (57⅔ x 45¼ in) (Tate Gallery, London). De Chirico invented Metaphysical painting. His works have a strange, magical atmosphere. The setting is unreal and time is suspended.

♦ **GIORGIO MORANDI**
Still Life, 1919, oil on canvas, 56.5 x 47 cm (22¼ x 18½ in) (Brera, Milan). Morandi took part in the Metaphysical painting movement for a few years, but then began his own personal study of how to represent the volume of objects, painting mostly still lifes.

♦ **MORANDI'S STYLE**
Giorgio Morandi, *Still Life*, 1921, oil on canvas, 60.5 x 66.5 cm (23¾ x 26¼ in) (Private collection, Milan). Morandi portrayed objects as though they had been arranged on a theater stage. By use of subtle shades, he conveyed a sense of the volumes of objects within a space.

♦ **MAX ERNST**
After Us, Motherhood, 1927, oil on canvas, 146.5 x 114.5 cm (57⅔ x 45 in) (Kunstsammlung Nordrhein-Westfalen, Düsseldorf).

♦ **SURREALISM**
This movement in art and literature was founded in 1924 by the French writer André Breton. The idea was to show the "super-real" world of dreams, rather than just the everyday real world. The Surrealists claimed Picasso as one of their own. At the first Surrealist exhibition in Paris in December 1925, there were works by Picasso and other artists including Giorgio de Chirico (1888-1978), the Italian inventor of Metaphysical painting; the Swiss Paul Klee (1879-1940), one of the greatest twentieth-century artists; Max Ernst (1891-1976), the most important German Surrealist; and the Spanish Joan Miró (1893-1983), who created a visual universe populated by mysterious symbols resembling microscopic organisms.

♦ **JOAN MIRÓ**
Dutch Interior II, 1928, oil on canvas, 92 x 73 cm (36¼ x 28¾ in) (Peggy Guggenheim Collection, Venice).

♦ **AVANT-GARDE PICASSO**
Pablo Picasso, *The Dance*, 1925, oil on canvas, 215 x 142 cm (84⅔ x 56 in) (Tate Gallery, London). Here was a new way of representing the human figure, exemplifying the courage and genius of Picasso, the avant-garde artist.

♦ **TRADITIONAL PICASSO**
Pablo Picasso, *Paulo as Pierrot*, 1925, oil on canvas, 130 x 97 cm (51 x 38 in) (Picasso Museum, Paris). At the same time as he painted innovative works, Picasso also worked on traditional portraits.

PLAYING WITH THE HUMAN FORM

In a series of paintings of bathers on a beach, Picasso subjected the human body to a total transformation. The arms, legs and heads of the figures are excessively elongated, so that they take on the bizarre proportions of unrecognizable creatures that might be from a dream. Painted to look like enormous sculptures, these figures were the closest Picasso ever came to Surrealism.

♦ THE WORKS
Between 1928 and 1930, Picasso painted a series of portraits which were all very similar, both in subject matter and in the shades of color he used. In the main, these works were painted during the summer months, most of them in Dinard, a seaside town on the coast of Brittany. The canvases were almost always small, and together form a cycle of Picasso's work which is known as *Bathers*. The preparatory drawings that Picasso made for this series are found in his exercise book, *Carnet 95*. This shows that Picasso began the studies during the summer of 1927, while he was staying in Cannes. The two paintings in this column can also be traced back to this creative phase. Top: *The Swimmer*, 1929, charcoal and oil on canvas, 162 x 130 cm (63³/₄ x 51 in) (Picasso Museum, Paris). Below: *The Acrobat*, 1930, oil on canvas, 162 x 130 cm (63³/₄ x 51 in) (Picasso Museum, Paris).

THE STUDIO ♦
Picasso in 1928. Some examples of his *Bathers* series, painted in Dinard, can be seen on the floor of his studio.

11. PICASSO'S LIFE ♦ *Picasso continued to sell his work successfully. In spite of the worldwide depression from 1929, his earnings did not fluctuate. During the early 1930s many artists had serious financial problems and the gallery owner Daniel-Henri Kahnweiler set up a fund from which his painters were paid allowances that enabled them to survive. Picasso, on the other hand, had accumulated considerable wealth and, even at this time, was able to buy the eighteenth-century château of Boisgeloup, about 70 kilometers (43 miles) from Paris. It was a spacious home, with about twenty rooms, a Gothic chapel and a large, round pigeon-loft. Picasso especially enjoyed the stables, a row of buildings where he set up studios for sculpture and graphic work. With the help of the sculptor Julio González he began to produce a series of sculptures in metal. He threw himself into his work to avoid the continuing arguments with Olga.* ➤

ON THE BEACH ♦
Pablo Picasso, *Football Players on the Beach*, 1928, oil on canvas, 24 x 34.9 cm (9¹/₂ x 13³/₄ in) (Picasso Museum, Paris).

TRANSFORMATION ♦
Pablo Picasso, *Figure*, 1928, metal wire and sheet-metal, 50.5 x 18.5 x 40.8 cm (20 x 7¹/₄ x 16 in) (Picasso Museum, Paris). The human figure is represented as a series of points joined by lines.

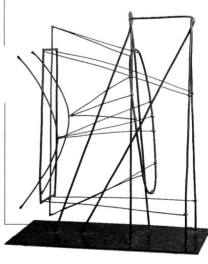

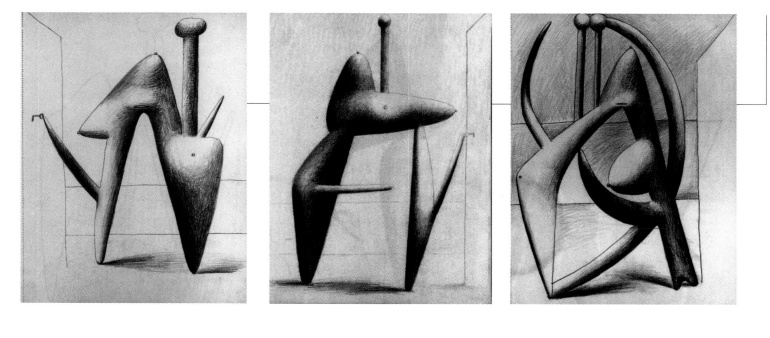

♦ **CARNET 95**
Pablo Picasso, *Pages 91, 92 and 94*, 1927, pencil on paper, 30.3 x 23 cm (12 x 9 in) (Picasso Museum, Paris). The human body has been distorted into extraordinary shapes in these drawings.

♦ **PROPORTIONS**
Pablo Picasso, *Bathers on the Beach*, 1928, oil on canvas, 21.5 x 40.4 cm (8½ x 16 in) (Picasso Museum, Paris). The figures on the beach are gigantic in relation to the background.

♦ **A SCULPTED APPEARANCE**
In this painting entitled *Bather*, 1928, oil on canvas, 22 x 14 cm (8⅔ x 5½ in) (Picasso Museum, Paris), the body is made up of elements that have the solidity of sculpture.

FROM DRAWING TO SCULPTURE ♦
Pablo Picasso, *Bather (Metamorphosis II)*, a sculpture from 1928, 23 x 18 x 11 cm (9 x 7 x 4⅓ in) (plaster original, Picasso Museum, Paris). This three-dimensional work was also based on drawings in *Carnet 95*.

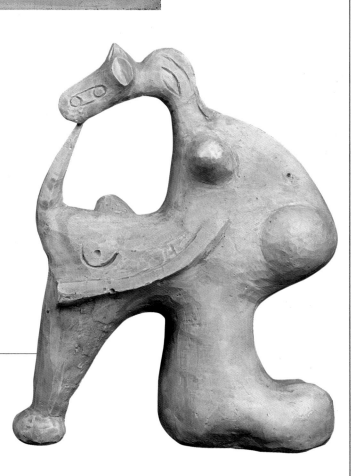

PICASSO'S VIEW OF WOMEN

During the late 1930s Picasso developed an original idea of the portrait, as reflected in a series of paintings from that time. These works were the outcome of the artist's detailed study of how the human form could be manipulated. They show how Picasso combined features from two lines of research: Cubist-style dissociation, where the subject is portrayed from various points of view at the same time; and children's drawing with its great freedom of composition.

♦ **PORTRAITS OF WOMEN**
The human figure was a central theme of all of Picasso's work and he focused especially on portraits of women. At first, he chose his subjects from members of his family, as in *Portrait of Aunt Pepa*, above, 1896, oil on canvas, 57.5 x 50.5 cm (22²/₃ x 20 in) (Picasso Museum, Barcelona), painted in an impeccable academic style. During the Blue Period, he painted ballerinas and prostitutes, as in *Woman in a Chemise*, center, 1905, oil on canvas, 73 x 59.5 cm (28³/₄ x 23¹/₂ in) (Tate Gallery, London). These were still realistic likenesses. With the emergence of Cubism, such representations were replaced by distorted views.
Below: *Portrait of Gertrude Stein*, detail, 1905-1906, oil on canvas, 99.6 x 81.3 cm (39¹/₄ x 32 in) (Metropolitan Museum of Modern Art, New York).

♦ **DISSOCIATION**
Pablo Picasso, *Woman in a Striped Hat*, 1939, oil on canvas, 81 x 54 cm (32 x 21¹/₄ in) (Picasso Museum, Paris).

Not only have the front and side views of the face been superimposed on each other, but also the face has been twisted along a series of parallel lines.

♦ **DOUBLE VISION**
Pablo Picasso, *Portrait of Dora Maar*, 1937, oil on canvas, 55.3 x 46.3 cm (21³/₄ x 18¹/₄ in) (Picasso Museum, Paris). The woman is portrayed at once from the front and the side, in non-realistic color. The image is true only to Picasso's own vision.

♦ **FRAGMENTATION**
Pablo Picasso, *Lady in a Straw Hat*, 1936, oil on canvas, 61 x 50 cm (24 x 19²/₃ in) (Picasso Museum, Paris). The eyes are placed at opposite sides of a face floating in the center of the picture.

12. PICASSO'S LIFE ♦ *Picasso's marriage finally broke up at the beginning of 1935; Olga left, taking their son Paulo with her. Proceedings for legal separation began, which the artist found distressing. At this point his old friend Jaume Sabartès came to Paris to help him and remained as his secretary for the rest of his life. In addition to Sabartès' company, the birth of Picasso's first daughter, Maya, from his relationship with Marie-Thérèse, also brought him comfort. When the Spanish Civil War began in July 1936, Picasso declared his opposition to General Franco and his allegiance to the Republican government. In August of that year, in Mougins, near Cannes, he met the Yugoslavian photographer, Dora Maar, and she became his new companion.* ➡

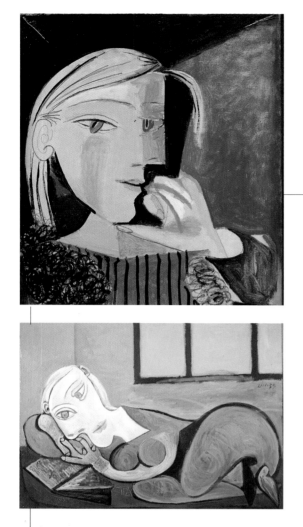

♦ WOMEN PICASSO PAINTED
As the years went by, Picasso more often used the women with whom he was amorously involved as the subjects of his portraits. Examples are *Woman Seated (Dora Maar)*, top, 1941, oil on canvas, 99.8 x 80.5 cm (39¹⁄₃ x 31²⁄₃ in) (Private collection) and *Portrait of Jacqueline Roque with Hands Folded*, center, 1954, oil on canvas, 116 x 88.5 cm (45²⁄₃ x 35 in) (Picasso Museum, Paris). Throughout his working life, Picasso continued to

♦ VARIATIONS
These three paintings show Picasso's ability to create different versions of the same subject. Top: *Portrait of Marie-Thérèse Walter*, 1937, oil on canvas, 46 x 38 cm (18 x 15 in). Above: *Woman Reclining Reading (Marie-Thérèse Walter)*, 96.5 x 130.5 cm (38 x 51¹⁄₃ in). Above right: *Portrait of Marie-Thérèse Walter*, 1937, oil on canvas, 100 x 81 cm (39¹⁄₃ x 32 in). (All three paintings, Picasso Museum, Paris).

♦ METAMORPHOSIS
Pablo Picasso, *Woman's Head*, 1939, oil on canvas, 65 x 54.5 cm (25¹⁄₂ x 21¹⁄₂ in) (Picasso Museum, Paris). The artist changed the symmetrical structure of the face so much that it became unrecognizable.

♦ SORROW
Pablo Picasso, *Weeping Woman*, 1937, oil on canvas, 60 x 49 cm (23²⁄₃ x 19¹⁄₄ in) (Tate Gallery, London). The distorted expression was produced by breaking up and reassembling the parts of the face.

explore ways of representing the female form. In his portraits it can be seen to undergo a process of metamorphosis. Examples from his later years, such as *Great Profile*, below, 1963, oil on canvas, 130 x 97 cm (51 x 38 in) (Kunstsammlung Nordrhein-Westfalen, Düsseldorf) convey a sense of confident authority.

GUERNICA

On 26 April 1937, during the Spanish Civil War, an aerial attack by Nazi bombers acting as allies of the Spanish fascists completely destroyed the Basque town of Guernica in north-east Spain. The horror of the event was described by Picasso in his painting, entitled *Guernica*, which he started immediately and finished within a month. The work reveals Picasso's deeply-held belief in freedom for all, which led him to take the part of the oppressed and victims of violence. In spite of its title, the painting does not contain any specific details that tie it to the actual bombing of Guernica. It is a symbol of the devastation caused by all war. By not including any precise references to the particular event, Picasso gave the painting a universal significance: its message is that all war is madness.

♦ AN HISTORIC PAINTING
Civil war broke out in Spain in 1936. The two opposing sides were the Republican government of the Popular Front, democratically elected, and the fascist Falange under the command of General Franco, aided by Mussolini and Hitler. In January 1937 the Popular Front asked Picasso to create a work for the Spanish Pavilion at the Paris International Exhibition, which was to open in July. Picasso accepted the commission and planned a work which would show an artist in his studio, painting from a life model. However, news of the bombing of Guernica prompted him to create a painting that was totally different from that first idea.

THE STUDIO ♦
The studio where Picasso painted *Guernica* was in a seventeenth-century building in rue des Grands-Augustins, Paris. Here he had the use of huge rooms on the two top floors, with windows overlooking a courtyard.

ANIMAL SYMBOLS ♦
The bull and the horse, traditionally connected with the bullfight, symbolize the Spanish victims of oppression.

COLORS ♦
Picasso used only black, white and shades of grey to create a scene dominated by struggle and death.

♦ A SURREALIST VISION OF WAR
Salvador Dalí, *Premonition of Civil War or Soft Construction with Boiled Beans*, 1936, oil on canvas, 100 x 99 cm (39¹⁄₃ x 39 in) (Museum of Art, Philadelphia). This masterpiece of Surrealist art, dealing with the subject of war, was painted before the Spanish Civil War had broken out.

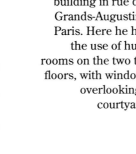

♦ **THE PAINTING OF THE CENTURY**
Pablo Picasso, *Guernica*, 1937, oil on canvas, 349.3 x 776.6 cm (137½ x 305¾ in) (Centro de Arte Reina Sofia, Madrid). Picasso made forty-five preparatory drawings and worked on six versions of the painting before producing the final one for the Paris International Exhibition, in July 1937.

♦ **MAX JACOB**
Picasso's great friend, the poet Max Jacob was a Jew. On 24 February 1944, he was arrested by the Nazis and taken to Drancy concentration camp. Despite a petition to save him, organized by Jean Cocteau, Jacob died a few days later.

♦ **DISTORTION**
Tormented by an oppressive force, all the figures are distorted, broken into irregular shapes.

♦ **THE SCREAM**
Humans and animals in the painting all have their mouths open to let out an enormous, collective scream of terror.

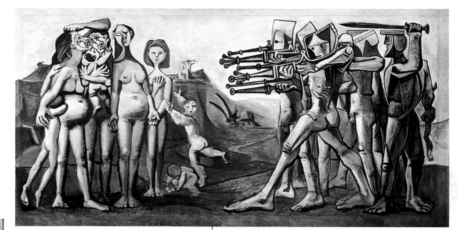

MASSACRE IN ♦ KOREA
Pablo Picasso, 1951, oil on canvas, 110 x 210 cm (43⅓ x 82⅔ in) (Picasso Museum, Paris).

DOVE OF PEACE ♦
A drawing made by Picasso for his daughter Paloma was chosen by Louis Aragon for the poster for the World Congress for Peace (Paris, 1949).

CONGRÈS MONDIAL
DES PARTISANS
DE LA PAIX
SALLE PLEYEL
20·21·22 ET 23 AVRIL 1949
PARIS

♦ **IN OCCUPIED PARIS**
It is said that during the Nazi occupation of Paris the German ambassador Abetz visited Picasso in his studio. On seeing a reproduction of *Guernica*, he asked the artist: "Did you do this?" – to which Picasso retorted: "No, you did."

13. PICASSO'S LIFE ♦ *Picasso set up a new studio in an old building in rue des Grands-Augustins in Paris. It was here that he painted* Guernica. *He also lived there during the Second World War, while Marie-Thérèse and Maya had an apartment on boulevard Henri-IV. When the Nazis occupied Paris, Picasso went into voluntary isolation, devoting his time mainly to painting and refusing any proposal that he should collaborate with the German invaders. He faced the difficulties of war, the cold, and constant uncertainty about what would happen to him and his loved ones with great spirit and determination. In the summer of 1944, when Paris was liberated from the Germans, Picasso was hailed as a symbol of anti-fascist resistance. In October he decided to join the French Communist Party – a move that gave rise to a great deal of public debate.* ➠

STILL LIFE WITH OX SKULL

When we look at this painting, our attention is drawn immediately to the center of the scene, where the animal's skull is set on a table in the foreground. The background is dark and divided into four equal-sized sections by the square wooden window frames. The two top sections are completely visible, while the bottom sections are partially obscured by the mass of the table.

♦**WOMAN IN TEARS**
Pablo Picasso, study for *Guernica*, 1937, drawing, 43 x 22 cm (17 x 8²/₃ in) (Centro de Arte Reina Sofia, Madrid).

♦**THE WORK**
Still Life with Ox Skull, 1942, oil on canvas, 130 x 97 cm (51 x 38 in) (Kunstsammlung Nordrhein-Westfalen, Düsseldorf). Picasso painted this work in April 1942, while Paris was under Nazi control. It was one of a series of paintings containing the image of a skull. During the same month, he also painted *Bull's Head on a Table*, oil on canvas, 116 x 89 cm (45²/₃ x 35 in) (Emilio Jesi Collection, Madrid). This is a very similar work, but has paler, lemon colors which create a lighter atmosphere. These works were finished quickly, during one of Picasso's periods of intense isolation. During such times he rarely left the studio where the war had obliged him to remain.

♦**SKULL**
Pablo Picasso, bronze, 25 x 21 x 31 cm (10 x 8¹/₄ x 12¹/₄ in) (Picasso Museum, Paris).

♦**SCRAP**
Pablo Picasso, *Head of a Bull*, 1943, original from a bicycle handle and saddle, 33.5 x 43.5 x 19 cm (13 x 17 x 7¹/₂ in) (Picasso Museum, Paris). A sculpture made from scrap.

♦**A LATER DEVELOPMENT**
Pablo Picasso, *Still Life with Skull, Sea Urchins and Lamp on a Table*, 1946, oil on plywood, 81 x 100 cm (32 x 39¹/₃ in) (Picasso Museum, Paris). This is a human skull.

SUFFERING ♦
Pablo Picasso, *Horse's Head*, 1937, oil on canvas, 65 x 92.1 cm (25¹/₂ x 36¹/₄ in) (Centro de Arte Reina Sofia, Madrid). A study for *Guernica*.

In Picasso's hands, "still life" becomes powerfully expressive. The dark colors give the painting a gloomy, threatening atmosphere, which reflects the fears and worries of wartime. The skull, suggesting silence, death and decay, is a symbol of uncertainty, impotence and the transience of life. The barred window, through which only dense, impenetrable darkness can be seen, creates an enclosed space like a prison cell, from which no-one can escape.

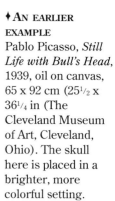

AN EARLIER EXAMPLE
Pablo Picasso, *Still Life with Bull's Head*, 1939, oil on canvas, 65 x 92 cm (25½ x 36¼ in (The Cleveland Museum of Art, Cleveland, Ohio). The skull here is placed in a brighter, more colorful setting.

THROUGH THE WINDOW
The view through the window is made up of vertical zones of color, with no realistic reference.

CUBISM
The ox's head is painted using a typically Cubist technique.

AN OPTICAL TRICK
The white areas at the base of the canvas, and also in the top right-hand corner, give greater depth to the whole scene.

THE TABLE
The table is also painted according to the ideas of Cubism, as a collection of surfaces slotting together.

LITHOGRAPHY

♦ **THE ORIGINS OF THE TECHNIQUE**
Lithography was invented in about 1796 by the German writer Aloys Senefelder and was introduced in France in about 1810 by Vivant de Non and André Offenbach. Great artists like Eugène Delacroix and Théodore Géricault used this process. When perfected, it became a method of production used mainly for newspapers in the nineteenth century. Above: a newspaper title page.

Lithography was popular in the early twentieth century and became so again after the Second World War. The technique involves drawing or painting an original design onto a stone or zinc plate with a special crayon or inks, fixing the image, then inking it and printing. The great advantage of the process is that it can be used to make hundreds of lithographs from one original. Clearly, the cost of a lithograph, even when it is produced with the greatest care to ensure the accuracy and excellence of the copy, is much less than the price of an original painting on canvas or paper. Lithographs thus made art available to people other than millionaire collectors. People who would never have been able to afford an original painting by Picasso were able to buy his lithographs. Picasso made great use of lithography to ensure that his work reached a wider market, and this is certainly one of the reasons why he achieved greater fame than any other artist before him.

♦ **VERSION ONE**
The Bull, 5 December 1945, 29 x 42 cm (11½ x 16½ in), pencil on stone.

VERSION FOUR ♦
The Bull, 22 December 1945, ink and scraping on stone.

LITHOGRAPHIC ♦ **STONE**
The artist draws directly onto a cleanly polished stone or zinc plate, using a purpose-made greasy crayon or lithographic ink. The subsequent process is based on the fact that grease repels water. The image is fixed with chemicals and the stone wetted. Then, when it is inked, only the image area, which has repelled the water, will accept the ink. At this point, paper is pressed on to the stone and a print is taken.

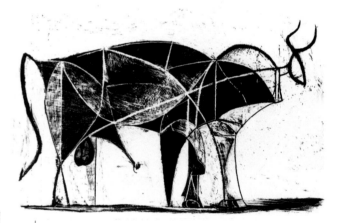

♦ **VERSION SEVEN**
The Bull, 28 December 1945.

VERSION TEN ♦
The Bull, 10 January 1946.

♦ **VERSION TWO**
The Bull,
15 December 1945,
crayon and ink on
stone.

VERSION FIVE ♦
The Bull, 24 December
1945, ink and scraping
on stone.

♦ **THE BULL**
When he became
interested in
lithography, Picasso
naturally found new
ideas and techniques
that he wanted to try
out. It was in the
studio of the best
lithographer in Paris,
Fernand Mourlot,
that he experimented
with different ways of
producing pictures of
The Bull. He started
by producing a
realistic print of a
bull with a solid body.
Then, as he
continued to
experiment, he
produced other
versions in which the
animal became more
and more stylized. In
the final stage it was
composed of just one
line. Another artist
would most likely
have stopped after
the first or second
version, but Picasso
was determined to
pursue his research
to the end.

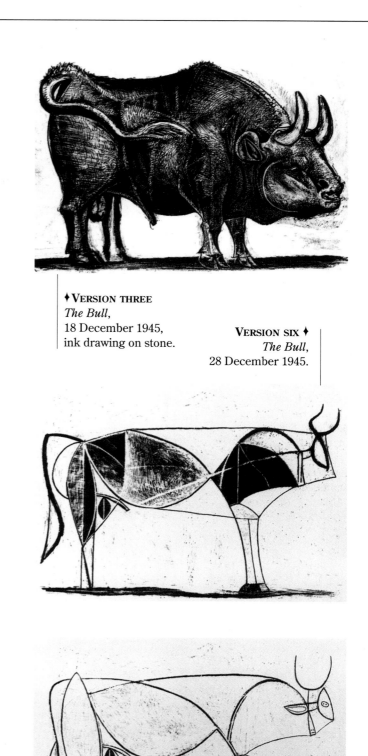

♦ **VERSION THREE**
The Bull,
18 December 1945,
ink drawing on stone.

VERSION SIX ♦
The Bull,
28 December 1945.

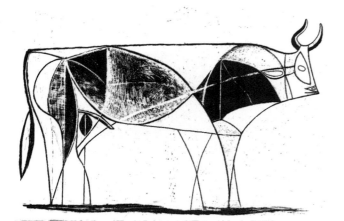

VERSION NINE ♦
The Bull, 5 January
1946.

♦ **VERSION EIGHT**
The Bull, 2 January
1946.

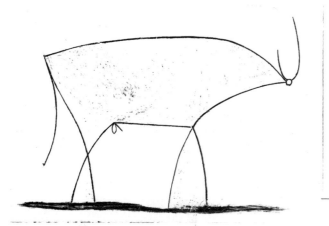

♦ **VERSION ELEVEN**
The Bull, 17 January
1946, ink drawing on
stone, 29 x 37.5 cm
(11½ x 14¾ in).

14. PICASSO'S LIFE ♦ *During the post-war period Picasso was tormented by his complicated love life. His relationship with Dora Maar was losing its importance for him since he had met and become very fond of an attractive young artist, Françoise Gilot. The situation caused Picasso and Dora to argue all the time. Perhaps to escape the dilemma in his personal life, Picasso began to work closely with the finest lithographer in Paris, Fernand Mourlot. In spring 1946, he decided to live with Françoise Gilot and they moved to Antibes for a number of months. The curator of the local museum allowed him to use rooms at the Grimaldi Palace as a studio, and the series of wall panels that Picasso left there bear witness to his happiness during this period. In 1947, his first child with Françoise, Claude, was born.* ⟫→

CERAMICS

Picasso worked with unique vigor and creativity in whatever medium he explored. In the late 1940s he became interested in ceramics, joining Georges and Suzanne Ramié in their workshop in Vallauris in the south of France. Having learned the basic techniques of pottery, he soon became dissatisfied with them. They seemed to inhibit him and so he invented and developed new ideas and methods, moving right away from what was traditional. To begin with, he made use of the usual, basic objects – plates, dishes and pots – which he decorated in his own innovative manner. Then, having become familiar with the material, he began to model pieces himself, using sculpting techniques to change the shape of soft, wet clay. Under his expert hand, pots and bottles were transformed into owls, pigeons and expressive female figures.

♦ **LEARNING FROM THE RAMIÉS**
Picasso first discovered the little town of Vallauris, near the Côte d'Azur, when he and Paul Eluard were out driving in 1936. Ten years later he met Georges and Suzanne Ramié, the directors of Madoura Ceramics, a factory in Vallauris. He joined them in their workshop, taking this opportunity to practice in a medium that was new to him. He started with no knowledge of how to shape clay, fire or decorate it. The Ramiés taught him all he needed to know to make his first ceramic pieces. From then on Picasso committed himself to this new venture with typical enthusiasm. At the time when he was most interested in ceramics, he produced over two thousand pieces in just one year.

♦ **THE SMILING PLATE**
Pablo Picasso, *"Face" Plate*, 30 May 1965, white ceramic, enamel slip decoration, diameter 25 cm (10 in) (Galerie Beyeler, Basel). By painting on just a few simple lines, Picasso produced a face that looks full of personality.

THE POTTER'S WHEEL ♦
Georges Ramié worked traditionally. He threw a ball of clay onto the wheel, started the wheel turning, and used his hands to model the material into the desired shape. Pots produced this way were always symmetrical.

♦ **A MADE-UP FACE**
Pablo Picasso, *"Face" Plate*, 20 June 1963, white ceramic, enamel slip, diameter 25 cm (10 in) (Galerie Beyeler, Basel). Picasso amused himself by applying heavy make-up to this plate, giving the face a puzzled expression.

♦ **THE FACE IN THE JUG**
Pablo Picasso, *"Woman's Face" Turned Jug*, 10 July 1953, white ceramic, decoration incised with knife and partly enamel slip, height 35 cm (13¾ in) (Galerie Beyeler, Basel). Picasso has decorated the jug to transform its shape into that of a woman's head.

♦ **SOFT CURVES**
Pablo Picasso, *"Polena" Turned Jug*, 1952, white ceramic, engraved and slip decoration, height 21 cm (8¼ in), width 24 cm (9½ in) (Galerie Beyeler, Basel). The decoration may be simple, but this does not take away from the elegance of the piece.

♦ **PICASSO'S METHOD**
Picasso used techniques from sculpture to model his pottery. For example, while the clay forming the neck of a pot was still wet, he pulled and twisted it into the shape of a pigeon. Using non-traditional methods like this, the great master of painting also produced ceramic pieces that were strikingly original.

♦ **TRANSFORMATION**
Pablo Picasso, *Bottle: Woman Kneeling*, 1950, China clay, turned on the wheel and modeled, decoration oxidized on white enamel, 29 x 17 x 17 cm (11½ x 6⅔ x 6⅔ in) (Picasso Museum, Paris). Picasso transformed the shape of the bottle into the figure of a woman deep in meditation.

15. PICASSO'S LIFE ♦ *In 1948 Picasso moved to Vallauris, where he was working with the ceramicist Georges Ramié. It was a small Provençal town, in a valley surrounded by pine forests, olive groves and vineyards. He lived there with Françoise Gilot and their baby son Claude. During a contented period he spent the mornings in the Ramiés' workshop and at lunchtime would go to the beach for a relaxing swim. In August 1948, he took part in the Congress of Intellectuals for Peace in Wrocław in Poland and also visited Auschwitz, the Nazi concentration camp. In April 1949, his and Françoise's second child, Paloma, was born. At about this time, too, he bought a studio at Vallauris, where he would work on sculptures. His relationship with Françoise became difficult and depression set in once more. Picasso was lifted from this by a secret liaison with the young Geneviève Laporte, which lasted until October 1953.* ➤♦

A FEMALE FIGURE ♦
Pablo Picasso, *Vase: Woman Wearing a Mantilla*, 1949, China clay, turned on the wheel and modeled, slip decoration, 47 x 12.5 x 9.5 cm (17½ x 5 x 3¾ in) (Picasso Museum, Paris). This vase was worked like a sculpture. The colors with which it is decorated give the figure its identity.

SCULPTURE

Picasso's work as a sculptor developed alongside his painting. In fact, often, the investigations he made in the field of painting led him to create three-dimensional works. He produced sculptures in a great multiplicity of forms, although many are alike, being made from simple material, such as cardboard, or waste and discarded objects. There is also one characteristic that underlies all his sculptures, from 1910 until the end of his career: that is his sense of humor. He regarded sculpture as a liberating and entertaining activity. Following his inspiration, he could manipulate and model the most unlikely and incompatible materials to invent surprising, playful representations of reality.

THE FOOTBALLER ✦
Pablo Picasso, 1961, cut and painted sheet-metal, 58.3 x 47.5 x 14.5 cm (23 x 18³/₄ x 5³/₄ in) (Picasso Museum, Paris). The painted areas identify the subject and the curves in the metal convey a sense of movement.

✦ GIRL SKIPPING
Pablo Picasso, 1950, original in plaster, parts from ceramic, wicker basket, kitchen tiles, shoes, wood and iron, 152 x 65 x 66 cm (60 x 25¹/₂ x 26 in) (Picasso Museum, Paris).

16. PICASSO'S LIFE ✦ *After the break-up of his relationship with Françoise Gilot, Picasso went through a period of solitude. He worked intently on a series of portraits of a young girl called Sylvette David. In 1954, he spent a pleasant summer holiday in Perpignan, where the sea, sun and visits to the bullfight acted like a tonic for him. During this time he established a close relationship with Jacqueline Roque, an assistant in the Ramiés' Vallauris workshop. A few months later she had become his new companion. He was deeply saddened by the deaths of Matisse and his first wife, Olga. Troubled and tired of being hounded by journalists and disturbed by a curious public, he left Paris and moved to "La Californie", a villa in Cannes. Here he regained his tranquillity and the concentration to paint. ⇒✦*

✦ THE STUDIO
In 1949 Picasso bought an abandoned perfume factory at Vallauris. He turned the dilapidated building into two painting studios and a third spacious one for making ceramics and sculptures and to use as a store-room.

A STAND ✦
While work was in progress, the goat's underbelly was supported by piles of bricks.

♦ PICASSO AND GOAT
Picasso loved animals, playing with them and using them as subjects for his sculpture.

FOUND OBJECTS ♦
Many of Picasso's sculptures were made by assembling an assortment of found objects. Everyday items and waste materials were glued together with plaster. An example is *The Goat*, 1950, 120.5 x 72 x 144 cm (47¹⁄₂ x 28¹⁄₃ x 56²⁄₃ in) (Picasso Museum, Paris).

♦ GETTING THE SHAPE
Picasso obtained the precise shape of the animal by arranging ceramic pots, bits of metal and wood, a palm frond, cardboard and plaster around a wicker basket, which gave a rounded shape for the underbelly.

♦ A BRONZE COPY
A bronze was cast from the plaster original. 120.5 x 72 x 144 cm (47¹⁄₂ x 28¹⁄₃ x 56²⁄₃ in) (Picasso Museum, Paris).

SURREALIST ♦ METHOD
Pablo Picasso, *Baboon and Young*, 1951, original made from a jug, two toy cars, metal and plaster, 56 x 34 x 71 cm (22 x 13¹⁄₃ x 28 in) (Picasso Museum, Paris). The idea for this sculpture came from two small toy cars which the gallery owner Kahnweiler gave to Picasso's son, Claude.

♦ PLASTER
Plaster is the simplest of all materials to use for sculpture. When work begins, it is wet and easy to model. Once dry, it is easy to carve.

PICASSO'S COURT AND THE BULLFIGHT

By the 1950s, Picasso had become famous throughout the world. He took refuge from the consequences of this celebrity at La Californie, his large villa in the hills above Cannes. Here he invited old and faithful friends, picking up the threads of the company he had enjoyed during the Barcelona "tertulia" years. Among the guests at La Californie were Daniel-Henri Kahnweiler, the ever-loyal Jaume Sabartès, Michel and Louise Leiris, Tristan Tzara and the poet Jacques Prévert. Picasso reigned over his friends like a king over his court. When he was not working or receiving the many visitors who came to see him, he went to the bullfight, always his favorite form of entertainment. He traveled at the head of a convoy. His older children, his nephew Janvier and old friend Totote Hugué accompanied him in his car, which was followed by the rest of his "courtiers".

♦ AT HOME
Picasso used the spacious rooms of La Californie as living quarters, as a studio where he practiced all forms of art, and as a private museum for his collection of works from the past. Chaos came to reign in the beautiful bright rooms, which were cluttered with masses of objects: cases of books, clothes piled up in the corners, old newspapers, and strangely-shaped lamps.

♦ LA CALIFORNIE
The large villa, built in Belle Epoque style, had belonged to the Moët champagne producer. It was situated in the hills above Cannes and surrounded by parkland. The idea was that its isolation would protect Picasso from prying eyes; but it was still not easy to avoid public attention.

Disorder was a feature of all Picasso's houses where wife, children, animals, friends, paintings, sculptures and souvenirs of all kinds combined to create an atmosphere buzzing with life, reflecting the artist's personality. When he was working, Picasso needed tranquillity and silence, but when he had finished work, he loved to socialize and enjoyed good company and the sound of conversation.

♦ PICASSO'S CAR
At age seventy, Picasso still enjoyed making long trips in his old yet still beautiful Hispano-Suiza.

AT THE BULLFIGHT ✦
The bullfight held an attraction for Picasso which he found irresistible. Here he was photographed at the bullfight at Nîmes, along with his wife Jacqueline Roque and his friend Jean Cocteau.

A PASSION SINCE ✦ CHILDHOOD
Pablo Picasso, *Bullring and Pigeons*, c. 1890, detail, pencil on paper, 13.5 x 20.2 cm (5⅓ x 8 in) (Picasso Museum, Barcelona). Aged nine, Picasso recorded the strong impression made on him by a bullfight he had watched with his father.

✦THE VIOLENCE OF THE BULLFIGHT
Pablo Picasso, *Bullfight: Death of the Toreador*, 1933, oil on board, 31.2 x 40.3 cm (12⅓ x 16 in) (Picasso Museum, Paris). Death is an inevitable part of bullfighting. Picasso represents it in an almost fairytale manner, to make the scene less harsh. The bull, horse and toreador are united in a seemingly happy embrace.

✦THE CONVOY
A black Bentley, containing Cocteau, other friends and the artist's secretary, followed Picasso's Hispano-Suiza.

LUIS MIGUEL ✦ DOMINGUIN
Picasso and this famous bullfighter became close friends in the 1950s because of their love of the corrida. It was a typically Spanish tradition that always reminded the artist of his childhood.

✦THE BULLFIGHT
Pablo Picasso, *Muleta: Movement with Cape*, 1957, drypoint, 20 x 30 cm (8 x 12 in), Block 967. Picasso dedicated many works to his favorite form of entertainment.

17. PICASSO'S LIFE ✦ *In January 1958 Picasso, in his seventies, finished a large mural for the Paris headquarters of UNESCO. His fame was growing to the point where he was constantly badgered by inquisitive crowds who gathered outside his villa in Cannes in the hope of meeting him. To try to escape from this type of attention, he moved to Vauvenargues, an ancient and imposing château in Provence, near Mont Sainte-Victoire, the subject of many paintings by Cézanne. The château was surrounded by 800 hectares (1977 acres) of parkland. In 1961 he married Jacqueline Roque, at a small ceremony attended by his closest friends. In the same year he decided to move to a country estate, "Notre Dame de Vie", in Mougins, 10 kilometers (6 miles) from Cannes. This house was more comfortable than the château and provided the tranquillity Picasso needed to work.* ➤

THE GUGGENHEIMS

At first, works by modern artists were bought by a minority of unconventional collectors who were far ahead of their time in appreciating new forms and styles. But in the second half of the twentieth century the market for modern art changed dramatically. Instead of those early collectors, businessmen often bought the paintings and sculptures, not just for their own personal enjoyment, but also in the hope that they were making a good financial investment. New buildings designed to house works of contemporary art were constructed in every large city in the world. Foundations were established to organize international exhibitions, and specialist modern art magazines began to be published. Public awareness of art was greater than ever before. The Guggenheim Museum of Art in New York, shown here, is an example of a museum which grew from one large private collection.

♦ **THE COLLECTOR**
Solomon Guggenheim was one of seven heirs to a family estate which, at the time of the First World War, included mines, foundries, a merchant fleet and banking interests. He was an art lover who, for years, collected paintings by Picasso, Kandinsky, Braque and many others. Guggenheim asked the architect Frank Lloyd Wright to design a museum to house his modern art collection. The building of the Guggenheim Museum of Art in New York City began seven years after the death of its founder, in 1956.

♦ **THE ARCHITECT**
American Frank Lloyd Wright (1867-1959) was one of the greatest architects of the twentieth century. In his design for the Guggenheim Museum, instead of the traditional arrangement of floors, he invented a spiral structure. On entering the building, visitors take an elevator to the top, and then view the museum by descending along ramps. The visit ends on the ground floor, near the exit. This was a revolutionary idea, to make the building more convenient.

♦ **BUILDING THE GUGGENHEIM**
Digging began on 16 August 1956. When Wright died in April 1959, the building work was almost complete. All that remained was to add the finishing touches. Six months later, on 21 October, the museum was opened to the public.

♦ **LIGHTING**
The lighting system is recessed to illuminate the paintings without dazzling the viewer.

♦ PICASSO AT THE GUGGENHEIM MUSEUM
Pablo Picasso, *Landscape at Céret*, 1911, oil on canvas, 65.1 x 50.3 cm (25²/₃ x 19³/₄ in) (Solomon R. Guggenheim Museum, New York). A work from the Cubist period, originally part of Solomon Guggenheim's private collection.

PABLO PICASSO ♦
Guitar and Glass on a Table, 1913, pencil on paper, 11 x 17.5 cm (4¹/₃ x 7 in) (Picasso Museum, Paris).

♦ THE ELEVATOR
The elevator carries people to the top floor, where the museum visit begins.

♦ THE RISE IN PRICE OF A PICASSO
In 1900 Pedro Mañach, the owner of the first gallery to accept Picasso's paintings, paid the artist 150 francs per month for all the works he could produce. At this time, a good meal in a restaurant cost about 3 francs.
In 1912, in the middle of the Cubist period, a London gallery sold works by Picasso at prices ranging between £2 and £22 sterling ($10-$100). During the 1920s prices began to rise considerably. At an auction held by the gallery owner Wilhelm Uhde, thirteen paintings sold for a total of 65,000 francs. After the Second World War, Picasso's works came to be collected by the world's most important museums. Consequently, their value rose sharply. During the 1960s, a noted portrait cost £32,000 and a Cubist painting fetched $500,000. Picasso's works are now some of the most expensive in art history. A small drawing may fetch hundreds of thousands of dollars and an oil painting could easily be valued in the millions.

PABLO PICASSO ♦
Dead Birds, 1912, oil on canvas, 46 x 65 cm (18 x 25¹/₂ in) (Prado, Madrid).

LESSONS LEARNED FROM OLD MASTERS

Picasso was a revolutionary painter who overturned the most widely accepted traditions and practices of art. At the same time, however, he always paid great attention to art history, studying works from the past and taking from them elements that could help him develop his own perceptions. In his earlier paintings, his interest in the old masters is evident mostly in stylistic effects which he borrowed from them and incorporated into his own work in a completely original way. After 1950, he began a more direct "dialogue" with the painters of some of the most famous works in the history of art. Using his own style, he painted variations on works by Velázquez, Courbet, David, El Greco and Delacroix. While, on the one hand, he was paying homage to past art, on the other, he was taking possession of this legacy and imposing on it his own unmistakable style.

♦ **DAVID**
Above: Jacques-Louis David, *The Rape of the Sabines*, 1799, oil on canvas, 386 x 520 cm (152 x 204³/₄ in) (Louvre, Paris).
Below: Pablo Picasso, *The Rape of the Sabines (after David)*, 1962, oil on canvas, 97 x 130 cm (38 x 51 in) (Georges Pompidou Center, Paris). Picasso keeps the warrior with his shield and the fighters in the foreground.

♦ **MANET**
Right: Pablo Picasso, *Déjeuner sur l'Herbe (after Manet)*, 1960, oil on canvas, 129 x 195 cm (50³/₄ x 76³/₄ in) (Picasso Museum, Paris). Here the Spanish artist was exploring a modern French masterpiece, Edouard Manet's, *Déjeuner sur l'Herbe*, left, 1863, oil on canvas, 208 x 264.5 cm (82 x 104 in) (Musée d'Orsay, Paris).

♦ **VELÁZQUEZ**
Left: Pablo Picasso, *Las Meninas (after Velázquez)*, 1957, oil on canvas, 194 x 260 cm (76¹/₃ x 102¹/₃ in) (Picasso Museum, Barcelona). Below: Diego Velázquez, *Las Meninas* (The Maids of Honor), 1656, oil on canvas, 318 x 276 cm (125 x 108²/₃ in) (Prado, Madrid). Picasso was fascinated by the work of the great Spanish master.

COURBET ♦
Above: Gustave Courbet, *Young Girls on the Banks of the Seine*, above, 1857, oil on canvas, 173.5 x 206 cm (68¹/₃ x 81 in) (Musée du Petit Palais, Paris). Right: The women become intertwined Cubist shapes in Picasso's *Young Girls on the Banks of the Seine (after Courbet)*, 1950, oil on plywood, 100.5 x 201 cm (39¹/₂ x 79 in) (Öffentliche Kunstsammlung, Kunstmuseum, Basel).

POETS AND PICASSO

Picasso was always interested in literature and many of his closest friends were well-known poets and writers. During his early days in Paris, Max Jacob introduced him to the capital's most stimulating cultural circle, as well as teaching him the rudiments of the French language. In the Cubist period, Guillaume Apollinaire was the strongest supporter of Picasso's new art. Picasso's entry into the world of theater was sponsored by Jean Cocteau. His friendship with André Breton, the founder of Surrealism, led Picasso to explore new ways of representing the human figure, daringly distorting it. Paul Eluard was a close confidant during the Second World War, and Rafael Alberti helped him in the last years of his life. Picasso's development as an artist could therefore be said to have been always under the guiding hand of poetry. And he was himself an accomplished poet.

♦ MAX JACOB
Max Jacob's first success was his autobiographical novel *Saint Matorel*, 1911. He later concentrated on poetry, using language full of complex religious references. Above: Pablo Picasso, *Max Jacob*, graphite, 32.6 x 25.3 cm (13 x 10 in) (Private collection).

♦ JEAN COCTEAU
Cocteau's talent took many forms and he was involved in several of the arts. Works for the theater such as *Orpheus*, 1927, and *Antigone*, 1928, gave a modern interpretation to Greek myths. His novel, *Les Enfants Terribles*, 1929, was an effective criticism of modern society.

♦ GUILLAUME APOLLINAIRE
Apollinaire was a writer and critic. In his collections *Alcools*, 1913, and *Calligrammes*, 1918, he created a style that combined mundane aspects of real life with literary allusions. He is best known for breaking down the boundary between prose and poetry. Below: Pablo Picasso, *Academician Apollinaire*, 1905, pen, ink and water-color on paper, 22 x 12 cm (8²⁄₃ x 4³⁄₄ in) (Picasso Museum, Paris).

1

2

♦ PORTRAITS
1. Max Jacob (1876-1944).
2. Guillaume Apollinaire (1880-1918).
3. Jean Cocteau (1889-1963).

4. André Breton (1896-1966).
5. Paul Eluard (1895-1952).
6. Rafael Alberti (born 1902 in Puerto de Santa Maria).

♦ INTELLECTUALS
On 16 June 1944 everyone who had taken part in his farce, *Desire Caught by the Tail*, was invited to Picasso's studio in rue des Grands-Augustins. The most eminent intellectuals in Paris were there. From the left, standing: Jacques Lacan, Cécile Eluard, Pierre Reverdy, Louise Leiris, Zanie Aubier, Picasso, Valentine Hugo, Simone de Beauvoir; in front: Jean-Paul Sartre, Albert Camus, Michel Leiris, Jean Aubier.

18. PICASSO'S LIFE ♦ *Picasso's serene existence at Mougins was disturbed in 1965 by the publication of Françoise Gilot's memoirs. She described the artist as egotistical and insensitive. Picasso was enraged, and even broke with his children Claude and Paloma. In the next two years he suffered both emotionally and in his health. In 1966, his writer friend André Malraux, who had become Minister of Cultural Affairs, organized a retrospective exhibition of Picasso's work in Paris, showing over 700 works. Still energetic, Picasso continued to produce an enormous quantity of paintings. In 1971, the Louvre hosted an exhibition of his work, an honor not normally bestowed on a living artist. Aged 91, Picasso died at Mougins on 8 April 1973. He was buried in the parkland around the château of Vauvenargues.*

♦ GROUP PHOTO
Picasso with friends in 1944. From the left: De Zarate, Françoise

Gilot, Fenosa, Jean Marais, Pierre Reverdy, Picasso, Jean Cocteau, Brassai.

3   4   5   6

♦ **ANDRÉ BRETON**
Breton turned to literature from studying neuropsychiatry, and his work always touched on psychological themes: the artist's creative imagination, dreams, the functioning of the human mind. The founder of Surrealism, he wrote poetry and prose. *Nadja*, 1928, and *L'Amour Fou (Mad Love)*, 1937, are among his greatest works.

♦ **PAUL ELUARD**
Eluard was the greatest of the Surrealist poets. His compositions combined light and shade, delirious thoughts and musical rhythms, as in the collection *Capitale de la douleur (Capital of Sorrow)*, 1926, dedicated to his wife.

♦ **RAFAEL ALBERTI**
Having begun with a poem full of social comment, Alberti, the only Spaniard in Picasso's group of poet friends, turned to Surrealism, with *Sobre los Àngeles (Concerning Angels)*, 1929. During the 1930s he lived in exile in France, Mexico, Argentina and Italy. His book *The Eight Names of Picasso*, 1970, was the result of his friendship with the artist.

Top: a woodcut for Apollinaire's *Bestiaire*. Below: a cover for his *Calligrammes*.

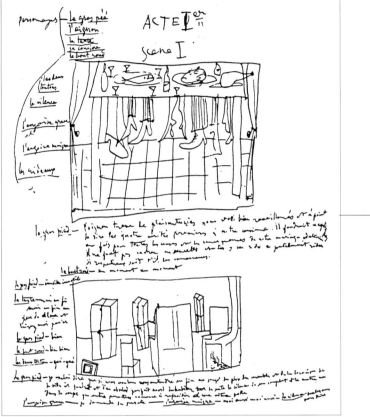

♦ **PICASSO THE BOOK ILLUSTRATOR**
Above left: the first page of the manuscript for the farce, *Desire Caught by the Tail*, designed in 1941. Above: illustration for *Grand Air* by Paul Eluard, 4 June 1936, etching, 41 x 31.5 cm (16 x 12½ in).

♦ **UBU-ROI**
In 1905 Picasso drew Ubu-Roi, an anarchic character created by Alfred Jarry in 1896. Pen and colored pencil on paper, 26.5 x 32.5 cm (10½ x 12¾ in) (Picasso Museum, Paris).

MAN AND WOMAN

The man and the woman are portrayed from mid-chest to the top of the man's hat which, although worn by him, covers both their heads. They dominate the canvas, positioned in the center. The faces are thrust so tightly together that the couple gives the impression of being a single creature rather than two distinct people. The whole scene is enveloped in a non-natural light, achieved by a violent mixture of grey and pink tones.

♦ **MOTHER AND CHILD**
Pablo Picasso, 1971, oil on canvas, 162 x 130 cm (63³/₄ x 51 in) (Picasso Museum, Paris).

♦ **THE WORK**
Man and Woman, 1971, oil on canvas, 116 x 88.5 cm (45²/₃ x 35 in) (Musée des Beaux-Arts, Nancy). This was painted during the month of July 1971, in the studio of the Notre Dame de Vie house near Mougins. The canvas is part of a group of works which Jacqueline Picasso donated to the French government, after her husband's death, for the establishment of the Picasso Museum in Paris. It is one of the finest examples of Picasso's painting style at the end of his life, when he experienced one of his most productive periods ever. In only 20 months, from September 1970 to June 1972, he painted two hundred and one works. The old master still had the energy of a young man and built up a surprising range of characters in these last works.

♦ **THE FAMILY**
Pablo Picasso, 1970, oil on canvas, 162 x 130 cm (63³/₄ x 51 in) (Picasso Museum, Paris).

♦ **ANOTHER COUPLE** ♦
Pablo Picasso, *The Kiss*, 1969, oil on canvas, 97 x 130 cm (38 x 51 in) (Picasso Museum, Paris). Again the two faces merge into one.

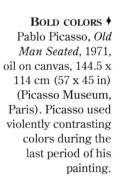

♦ **BOLD COLORS** ♦
Pablo Picasso, *Old Man Seated*, 1971, oil on canvas, 144.5 x 114 cm (57 x 45 in) (Picasso Museum, Paris). Picasso used violently contrasting colors during the last period of his painting.

At first sight, these figures seem to have been painted without regard for the conventional rules of representation, like the work of a child. However, further study of the painting's apparent crudeness brings home to the spectator Picasso's *extraordinary power of expression.* Man and Woman *is an aggressive and vibrant painting, created with vigorous brushstrokes and sudden explosions of energy.*

♦ **ABOVE THE HAT**
Pablo Picasso, *Man and Woman*, detail. The top edge of the painting is made up of rapid strokes of color.

♦ **SIMPLIFICATION**
Pablo Picasso, *Man and Woman*, detail. The hair is a series of simple lines.

♦ **CUBISM**
Pablo Picasso, *Man and Woman*, detail. The position of the noses makes the faces reminiscent of the Cubist-style portraits of the 1930s.

♦ **THE HANDS**
Pablo Picasso, *Man and Woman*, detail. The hands are deliberately not modeled, so that they look as though they have been cut out.

◆ KEY DATES IN PICASSO'S LIFE

1881	Birth of Pablo Ruiz Blasco Picasso, 25 October, in Málaga, Spain. According to Spanish custom, he takes the surnames of both parents.
1895	The Ruiz family moves to the Catalan city of Barcelona where Pablo's father has been appointed a drawing teacher at the School of Fine Arts.
1897	Pablo goes to Madrid and applies for entry to the Royal Academy of San Fernando, passing the exams with ease.
1900	Picasso's first exhibition is held at Els Quatre Gats, a tavern in Barcelona. In October Picasso leaves for Paris, with his friend Carlos Casagemas.
1901	Beginning of the Blue Period. For three years Picasso's work focuses on the homeless and social outcasts and is dominated by shades of blue.
1904	Picasso settles in Paris, living with other artists in an old building known as the Bateau Lavoir. Inspired by the circus, he begins his Rose Period.
1907	Picasso finishes a huge canvas on which he has been working secretly. *Les Demoiselles d'Avignon*, marking the start of Cubism, shocks even his friends.
1909	On vacation in Spain, Picasso paints many works which are exhibited when he returns to Paris. Cubism begins to gain recognition.
1914	France is at war with Germany. Many of Picasso's friends are drafted into the army. As a Spanish citizen, he is not involved and remains in Paris.
1917	The poet Jean Cocteau involves Picasso in a production of the ballet, *Parade*. Picasso meets Olga Koklova, a ballerina with the Diaghilev company.
1921	Having married in 1918, Picasso and Olga celebrate the birth of their son Paulo. Picasso is now famous and beginning to make money.
1928	For the next two years Picasso works on a series of paintings of bathers. These works are the closest that the artist comes to Surrealism.
1935	Olga leaves Picasso, taking Paulo with her. Several months later Picasso's daughter, Maya, is born, from his long-standing relationship with Marie-Thérèse Walter.
1936	Civil war breaks out in Spain. Picasso sides with the Republicans, the elected government, against General Francisco Franco and the Nationalists.
1937	On 26 April the Basque city of Guernica is destroyed by German bombers. Picasso's painting, *Guernica*, becomes a symbol of the devastation wreaked by war.
1939	Hitler invades Poland, causing France and England to go to war. Other nations become involved and the Second World War breaks out. The Nazis occupy France.
1944	The Allies invade Normandy in June and the liberation of Europe gets under way. Picasso is hailed as a symbol of resistance to Nazism.
1947	Picasso's third child, Claude, is born. His mother, Françoise Gilot, is Picasso's new companion, with whom he moves to the south of France.
1949	Although a daughter, Paloma, has been born, the relationship between Picasso and Françoise is at breaking point. They separate finally in 1953.
1954	Picasso buys a house near Cannes and lives there with his new companion, Jacqueline Roque. He is now very famous and harassed by a curious public.
1966	André Malraux, a writer friend appointed Minister of Cultural Affairs, organizes a retrospective exhibition of over 700 of Picasso's works.
1973	Death of Picasso, aged 91, on 8 April at Mougins. Two years earlier, the Louvre has hosted an exhibition of his work, an unusual honor for a living artist.

◆ WHERE TO SEE PICASSO'S WORK

Picasso's artistic career began when he was a child and continued throughout his long life. The large number of works he created can be found in many collections almost all over the world. The following list includes museums dedicated entirely to Picasso – like the Picasso Museums of Barcelona and Paris – and other important French, Spanish, British and American museums noted for the works by Picasso that they contain.

ENGLAND

LONDON, TATE GALLERY
As well as various female portraits such as *Woman in a Chemise* (1905); *Woman Weeping* (1925); and *Nude Woman in an Armchair*, one of Picasso's best-known works, *The Dance* (1925), is also exhibited here.

FRANCE

PARIS, PICASSO MUSEUM
In addition to numerous works donated by Picasso's heirs after his death, the museum houses many later acquisitions. This is one of the largest Picasso collections in the world. Among the paintings exhibited: *Celestina* (1904); *Tío Pepe and the Family of Saltimbanques* (1905); *Reading the Letter* (1921); *Family on the Seashore* (1922); *The Swimmer* (1929); *The Acrobat* (1930); *Portrait of Marie-Thérèse Walter* (1937); *Portrait of Jacqueline Roque with Hands Folded* (1954); *Le Déjeuner sur l'Herbe (after Manet)* (1960); *The Family* (1970). There are also preparatory studies for *Les Demoiselles d'Avignon*; various sculptures, including the bronze *Head of a Woman (Fernande)* (1909) and *Head of a Woman (Marie-Thérèse Walter)* (1931), the painted and cut-out sheet-metal *Footballer* (1961), the original *Goat*, in plaster and other materials (1950); and the series dedicated to the subject of bathers. Letters and photographs complete the museum's rich collection.

PARIS, GEORGES POMPIDOU CENTER
The curtain for the ballet *Parade*, painted in 1917, is exhibited in the Modern Art Museum in the Georges Pompidou Center building. Two other major works on show are *Violin* (1913-14) and *The Rape of the Sabines (after David)* (1962).

SPAIN

BARCELONA, PICASSO MUSEUM
The Catalan capital is where the young Picasso took his first steps as an artist, and many of his paintings are kept in two beautiful medieval buildings in the city's historic center. A large number were donated by the artist himself in 1968. In addition to works from his childhood – the pigeons and the bullfights that he drew when he was ten or eleven – there are many portraits of family and friends. Some were exhibited for the first time at Els Quatre Gats in 1900. The museum also houses some of the Blue and Rose Period paintings, *Woman in an Armchair* (1917) and the large painting, *Las Meninas (after Velázquez)* (1957).

MADRID, CENTRO DE ARTE REINA SOFIA
Guernica (1937), perhaps Picasso's most famous work, and many preparatory drawings and studies that were, until a few years ago, exhibited in an annex of the Prado Museum are now housed in this recently restored eighteenth-century building.

UNITED STATES

NEW YORK, METROPOLITAN MUSEUM OF ART
The Metropolitan's collection of works by Picasso includes a small self-portrait dated 1900; the *Portrait of Ramón Pichot* (1900); and the *Portrait of Gertrude Stein*, painted in Paris in 1905-6.

NEW YORK, MUSEUM OF MODERN ART
This museum houses *Les Demoiselles d'Avignon*, painted in 1907 and marking the beginning of Cubism. There is also the canvas entitled *Two Female Nudes* (1906); *Houses on a Hill*, painted in Horta de Ebro during the summer of 1909; *Harlequin* (1915); and *Three Musicians* (1921).

CLEVELAND (OHIO), CLEVELAND MUSEUM OF ART
La Vie, one of the most famous Blue Period works painted by Picasso in 1903, is housed here.

WASHINGTON (DC), NATIONAL GALLERY OF ART
This museum houses *The Family of Saltimbanques* (1905), considered the masterpiece of the Rose Period. It also contains portraits of Picasso's friend Pedro Mañach (oil on canvas) and first wife Olga Koklova (crayon and pencil on paper), painted in 1901 and 1929 respectively.

✦ LIST OF WORKS INCLUDED IN THIS BOOK

The works reproduced in this book are listed here, with their date (when known), the place where they are currently housed, and the number of the page on which they appear. The numbers in bold type refer to the credits on page 64.

Abbreviations:
W = whole; D = detail.
MOMA: Museum of Modern Art, New York;
MOP: Musée d'Orsay, Paris;
PCP: Georges Pompidou Center, Paris;
PMB: Picasso Museum, Barcelona;
PMP: Picasso Museum, Paris.

♦ INDEX

♦ CREDITS

The original and previously unpublished illustrations in this book may be reproduced only with the prior permission of Donati Giudici Associati, who hold the copyright. The illustrations are by: Simone Boni (pp 16–17, 22–23, 30–31, 34–35, 46, 50–51); L.R. Galante (pp 4–5, 6–7, 8–9, 10–11, 48–49, 52–53, 54–55).

Cover pictures, from top left: Alinari/Giraudon: 6, 24; Bridgeman Art Library: 7; Cleveland Museum of Art: 22; DoGi/Studiophot: 1, 2, 3, 4, 8, 9, 13, 21, 23; Edimedia: 18; Eric Lessing, Vienna: 11, 14; National Gallery, Washington: 17; Pompidou Center, Paris: 5, 12; RMN: 16, 20; Scala, Florence: 10, 19; Tate Gallery, London: 15.

DoGi s.r.l. have made every effort to trace copyright holders. If any omissions have been made, this will be corrected at reprint.
Alinari/Bridgeman/Giraudon: 185; Alinari/Giraudon: 2, 5, 8, 9, 13, 36, 38, 65, 72, 127, 163, 175, 181, 182, 187; Alinari/Lauros/Giraudon: 149; Artephot: 27;

Artephot/Held: 25; Artephot/Ideca: 165; Artephot/Musée Matisse, Nice: 33; Artephot/Oronoz: 3; Bridgeman Art Library: 12, 15, 16, 21, 39, 135, 177; Centro de Arte Reina Sofia, Madrid: 92; Cleveland Museum of Art, Cleveland, Ohio: 125; D.R.: 7; DoGi/Studiophot: 42, 52, 58, 59, 61, 63, 66, 67, 71, 77, 80, 85, 86, 90, 94, 97, 101, 105, 110, 111, 113, 118, 121, 126, 128, 134, 136, 150, 152, 154, 155, 156, 159, 162, 173, 176, 180; Edimedia: 17, 20, 23, 26, 29, 87; Eric Lessing, Vienna: 76, 171, 172; Galerie Beyeler, Basel: 56, 57, 99, 178; Kunstsammlung, Nordrhein-Westfalen, Düsseldorf: 64; Metropolitan Museum of Art, New York: 115, 122; Museo Arqueológico Nacional, Madrid: 4; Museum of Modern Art, New York: 73; Nasjonalgalleriet, Oslo: 40; National Gallery of Art, Washington: 30, 114, 151; Öffentliche Kunstsammlung, Basel: 131; Picasso Museum, Barcelona: 49, 75, 79, 83, 88, 98, 100, 104, 106, 107, 108, 109, 116, 117, 129, 167, 174; Picasso Museum, Paris: 1, 32, 50, 62, 96, 119, 160; Prado, Madrid: 53; RMN: 6, 18, 19, 41, 43, 44, 45, 46, 47, 48, 51, 54, 60, 68, 69, 70, 82, 84, 93, 95, 102, 112, 120, 123, 124, 130, 132, 133, 136, 137, 138, 139, 140, 142, 143, 144, 145, 146, 153, 161, 164, 166, 168, 169,

179; Scala, Florence: 24, 28, 34, 37, 55, 74, 81, 91, 103, 148, 157, 170, 183, 184; Scottish National Gallery of Modern Art, Edinburgh: 89; Serge Dominge/Marco Rabatti, Florence: 11, 31, 186; Solomon R. Guggenheim, New York: 78; Solomon R. Guggenheim Foundation, Venice: 10, 158; Staatens Museum for Kunst, Copenhagen: 22; Tate Gallery, London: 14, 35, 147.

Documents: (abbreviations: bc, bottom center; bl, bottom left; br, bottom right; c, center; cl, center left; cr, center right; t, top; tc, top center; tl, top left; tr, top right) Alinari/Giraudon: p 46tl; Archivio DoGi: pp 7tr, 11tr, 22tl, 22tr, 23tc, 23tr, 30tr, 34tr, 43cr, 52tl, 52tr, 54tr, 54cl, 54br; © Brassaï: 58c, 58br; Brian Brake/Rapho/Grazia Neri: 53tl; Collection Viollet: 11c, 14br, 23tl, 34cl, 53cr, 54tl, 59tr, 59br; Denis Brihat/Rapho/Grazia Neri: 51tl; Harlingue-Viollet: 4tl, 12tr, 34tl, 38tr, 43tr, 58tc, 58tr, 59tc(1), 59tc (3); Lipnitzki-Viollet: 14bl, 30tl, 30cl, 48tl, 59tl; L.L. Viollet: 11tl; Martinie-Viollet: 59tc (2); N.D. Roger Viollet: 8c; RMN: 21tr, 24c, 25tr, 28tr; Roger Viollet: 6tl, 6tr, 7tl, 10t, 11tc, 14tl.